بسم الله الرحمن الرحيم

Ḥanbali Fiqh of Worship

Five hundred most important issues expounded in a hundred and six questions and answers on Purification, Ṣalāt, Fasting, Zakāt & Ḥaj according to the school of Imām Aḥmad bin Ḥanbal

By Shaykh Mūsa bin ʿIsā Quddūmi Nābulsi

رحمه الله

Translated by Shaykh Khalid Shah

Ḥanbali Fiqh of Worship

A humble appeal is made to the readers for suggestions/corrections to improve the quality of this publication. May Allāh ta'āla reward you for this. The author, translators, editors, proof-readers and typesetters humbly request your du'ās for them, their parents, families, asātiza and mashāikh.

ISBN-13: 978-0-6482471-4-2

Published by:
Firdaws Academy Press
1830 Sydney Rd Level 2, Campbellfield
Victoria 3070, Australia
Web: www.firdawsacademy.org.au/press
Email: publications@firdawsacademy.org.au

Sketch of Nablus drawn by a traveller circa when author was residing and teaching there.

Arabic Transliteration Guide

Consonants						Short Vowels	
ء	a/i/u/’	ز	z	ق	q	ـَ	a
ب	b	س	s	ک	k	ـُ	u
ت	t	ش	sh	ل	l	ـِ	i
ث	th	ص	ṣ	م	m	**Long Vowels**	
ج	j	ض	ḍ	ن	n	ا ى	ā
ح	ḥ	ط	ṭ	ه	h	و	ū
خ	kh	ظ	ẓ	و	w	ي	ī
د	d	ع	‘	ى	Y	**Diphthongs**	
ذ	dh	غ	gh	ال	al- (article)	ـَو	aw
ر	r	ف	f	ة	a/at	ـَي	ay

Honorifics

ﷻ Jalla Jalāluhu – used to praise Allāh Ta‘āla – Meaning may His glory be exalted.

ﷺ Sallallāhu ‘alayhi wa sallam — Meaning “May Allāh bless him and give him peace.” Used for the Prophet Muḥammed ﷺ.

عَلَيْهِ السَّلَامُ / عَلَيْهَا السَّلَامُ / عَلَيْهِمُ السَّلَامُ ‘Alayhis salām— used following the mention of a prophet of Allāh, their family or angels translated as, “May the peace of Allāh be upon him/her/them.”

رَضِيَ اللهُ عَنْهُ / رَضِيَ اللهُ عَنْهُمْ / رَضِيَ اللهُ عَنْهَا Raḍiyallāho ‘anhu/‘anhum/‘anha —following the name of a companion(s) meaning “May Allāh be pleased with him/them/her.”

رَحِمَهُ اللهُ Raḥimahullāh – May Allāh Ta’lā have mercy on him - used for a pious person.

Foreword

All praise is due to Allāh, our creator, nourisher and provider. Peace and blessings be upon all the prophets and upon the last and final messenger Muḥammed ﷺ and peace and blessings be upon his companions who accepted and propagated Islām to the entire world.

Fiqh is from the noblest of sciences. It is a duty of every Muslim to learn fiqh, so that he may worship Allāh with knowledge. It is narrated by Muʿāwiyyah رضي الله عنه that Rasulullah ﷺ said: "Whoever Allāh intends goodness to, He gives him understanding of dīn."

Ibn Jawzī رحمه الله has said on the virtues of knowledge, that "it is a means of gaining recognition of the Creator and a means of remaining in the eternal bounty i.e. Jannah. There is no way of attaining nearness to Allāh Taʿāla except by knowledge and therefore it is a means of success in both worlds."

Imām Aḥmad bin Ḥanbal رحمه الله said that "knowledge does not become burdensome except for a jāhil (ignoramus)." This statement of the imām suffices as a censure of remaining ignorant.

Ḥasan Baṣri رحمه الله said that "when Allāh Taʿāla wants to humiliate a person, He deprives him of knowledge."

Ibn ʿAṭāullah رحمه الله said that "when Allāh Taʿāla gives you tawfīq to learn knowledge, know that He wants to give you knowledge."

About the book

This is a translation of Shaykh Quddūmi's رحمه الله booklet which covers five hundred of the most important masāil of worship. He was an authority on the Ḥanbali madhhab at the end of the 19th and beginning of the 20th century. The Abu Bakr Nūruddīn Tālib version of this text was used for the translation. He came upon the text in one of the old libraries of Damascus. His version is a new edition with layout improvements of the 1927 CE edition which was published in Syria by Shaykh Muḥsin Abdul Fattaḥ Al-Ḥajjawi An-Nabulsi Al-Ḥanbali رَحِمَهُ ٱللَّهُ.

The text appears to be based on another well-known foundational text i.e. *Dalīlut Tālib* of ʿAllāma Marʿī bin Yūsuf Al-Karmi Al- Ḥanbali (d. 1033 AH). This can be seen in the way the chapters and sections are divided and from what is listed as pre-requisites, wājibāt, arkān and sunnas of various actions.

Nūruddīn Tālib loved the way in which the masāil were presented in a simple language and a question-and-answer format which most students prefer. He explained in the foreword of the Arabic original, that this is an educational or teaching text and will greatly benefit as a *qāʿida* or primer to other texts of the Ḥanbali Madhhab such as *Dalīlut Talib* or *Zād ul Mustaqniʿ*.

About the translation

Alḥamdulillah and only with the tawfīq of Allāh Taʿāla, I have studied and taught this book several times both in English and Arabic. While studying this book with my late father Shaykh Gul Saeed Shah رَحِمَهُ ٱللَّهُ, and with his encouragement, I translated and published this book. This book was taught at Madrasah Islamiyyah Kāshiful Uloom (Melbourne, Australia) to first year kitāb students. It was taught in English in the first half of the year and then in Arabic in the second half. Kāshiful Uloom is a madrassa patterned on the the Darse Nizāmi syllabus.

On following a madhhab

The practices of Islam are transmitted to us in a complete form via the four madhhabs of the Ahlus Sunna wal Jamāʿah. They are the practical expression of the sharīʿa and Muslims have always adhered to one or the other, as they are the best articulation of Qurān and Sunnah. Views external to the four schools are considered fringe and unacceptable to Islamic scholarship for the last millennium and more. For those who want to understand why the Ahlus Sunna wal Jamāʿa strictly stick with in the four madhhabs may consult the translation of Ibn Rajab Al- Ḥanbali's

رَحِمَهُ ٱللَّهُ (d. 795 AH) treatise *Refutation of those who do not follow the four schools.*

Each madhhab has an intricate system that can deal with all human circumstances. That is why a supplement about the Ḥanbali madhhab is included with this translation for the readers benefit as an introduction to its history and inner workings.

Great Allāh-fearing imāms adhered to a single school and worked within its framework despite their genius and knowledge. Unfortunately, in this time, it has become a fashion in certain circles to reinvent the wheel and disregard their work, so they can offer their own interpretation. However, whatever new hybrid that will be produced, will be from people who neither possess the taqwa nor the depth of knowledge of the those imāms of the past.

The madhhabs also expose modernist trends, which seeks to change the dīn of Allāh based on external influences. The madhhabs are a great gift from Allah Taʿāla so that the orders of Allāh, are not compromised or changed due to social, economic or political pressures. Fiqh and specifically the rigorous system of a madhhab will state what is acceptable and what is unacceptable based on sound principles. They are rich and vast in scope to accommodate all scenarios and situations and provide guidance in all circumstances until Qiyāma.

Finally, we ask Allāh Taʿāla to benefit by means of this book and bless all those involved in bringing this work to publication with His countenance and to be near Him in the gardens of Jannah with His beloved slaves.

Khalid Shah

Madrasa Islamiyya Kāshiful Uloom

Melbourne, Australia

When Allāh ta'āla gives you tawfīq to learn knowledge, know that He wants to give you knowledge.

Ibn 'Aṭāullah

Contents

About the author 13

Chapter on ṭahārah (purification) 17

Section on Water 17

Rulings of containers and parts of carrion 19

Rulings of Siwāk 25

Rulings of masaḥ (wiping) on khuffs 35

Section on the invalidators of wuḍū 37

Section on ghusl (bathing) 41

Chapter on Ṣalāt 57

Section on Athān 57

Section on the ruling of ṣalāt 61

Section on the times of ṣalāt 63

Section on taṭawwuʿ (nafl prayers) 63

Section on the arkān (farḍ acts) of Ṣalāt 67

Wājibāt of Ṣalāt 71

Section on sujūd sahw 77

Joining two ṣalāts 91

Ṣalāt of janāza 103

Chapter on Fasting 109

Chapter on Zakāt 117

Chapter on Ḥaj 127

Appendices 135

Appendix 1: Biography of Imām Aḥmad bin Ḥanbal 137

Appendix 2 - Historical development & stages of the Ḥanbali school 147

Appendix 3: General principles of deriving rulings in the madhhab 155

Appendix 4: The most well-known works of the madhhab 166

Appendix 5: Some terminology used by the Ḥanbalis 173

الأحكام الخمسة

الواجب: وهو ما أُثيب فاعله، وعُوقب تاركه.

الحرام: ضد الواجب

المكروه: وهو ما أُثيب تاركه، ولم يعاقب فاعله.

المسنُون: هو ما أثيب فاعله، ولم يعاقب تاركه، والمكروه ضده.

المباح: الذي فِعْله وتركه سواء .

The Five Rulings

Legal Rulings are of five types. Upon them Islāmic jurisprudence is based. It is necessary to know them. They are:

1. **Wājib** or necessary – one is rewarded for performing it and is censured for omitting it (unless legally exempted).[1]
2. **Ḥarām** or unlawful – It is the opposite of wājib. The doer of ḥarām is punished and is rewarded for omitting it.
3. **Mandūb** or recommended - one is rewarded for doing but not punished for omitting. The highest form of mandūb is sunna and then faḍīla (virtue) and then nāfila (supererogatory).
4. **Makrūh** or offensive – It is the opposite of mandūb. That which one is rewarded for omitting but not punished for performing.
5. **Mubāḥ** or permissible - That which is free from praise and censure i.e. it has no reward or punishment.

---

[1] Wājib is generally understood to be synonymous with farḍ. However, in many masāil it is differentiated from wājib, where omission of farḍ will invalidate the action, while omission of a wājib can be excused if missed forgetfully or out of ignorance.

About the author[2]

Shaykh Mūsa bin ʿIsā was born in Qaddūm in 1849. Qaddūm lies fifteen kilometres west of Nablus, Palestine. Both Imām Bukhāri and Imām Muslim have narrated the ḥadīth of Rasulullah ﷺ in which Qaddūm is mentioned by name as the place where Ibrāhīm عليه السلام circumcised himself at the age of eighty. It was also a centre of Ḥanbalis in Shām (the Levant) and produced many great scholars. He was born to a pious family among whom his early education began. Nablus was the nearest metropolis to Qaddūm. This is where he spent most of his academic career.

He travelled to Damascus and studied with the likes of Sheikh Muḥammad and Sheikh Aḥmad the sons of Sheikh Ḥasan Shaṭṭi, Sheikh Sālīm ʿAṭṭār and Sheikh Bakri ʿAṭṭār.

After his studies he returned to Nablus and taught and trained ʿulamā with his cousin the erudite scholar Shaykh ʿAbdullah Ṣufān at the Madrasa of the Grand Ṣallaḥi Masjid. There he produced several books.

He was highly regarded and praised by his contemporaries. His biography says that he was a great research scholar with deep insight into many branches of knowledge. He was a mufassir, a muḥaddith, a jurist and grammarian. When Shaykh ʿAbdullah Ṣufān left for Hijāz in 1318 AH, Shaykh Mūsa became the focal-point of advanced studies for the whole of Nablus and surrounding region.

In the Syrian print of this book, he is referred to as "the author of this book the renown virtuous teacher, Shaykh Mūsa Effendi Al-Quddūmi Al-Nabulsi Al Hanbali..."

---

[2] His biography was summarised in the original Arabic from the following texts: Mukhtaṣar Tabaqāt Ḥanābila, Muḥammad Jamīl Shaṭṭi, pp. 215-216; Muʿjum Al-Muallifīn, Kaḥḥāla, vol. 3, p. 936; Muʿjum Buldān Falasṭīn, Muḥammad Ḥasan Shurāb, p. 626; Mulāḥiqan Naʿat Al-Akmal, Muḥammad Mutīʿ Al-Hāfiẓ, pp. 403-404; Dhaylud Dur Al-Munḍid, Ad-Dūsri, p. 103.

In 1331 AH, he was conferred with the title of *Izmīr* by the Ottoman Khalifa.

As Word War One broke out in 1332 AH, the Grand Ṣallaḥi Masjid was closed down and as a result the Shaykh's lessons ended there. However, he continued to teach till the end of his life.

It is said that, he passed away on the night of Laylatul Qadr in 1336 AH or 1908 CE.

May Allāh ta'āla be pleased with him and fill his grave with nūr. Āmīn.

كتاب الطهارة

باب المياه

الحمد لله وحده، والصلاة والسلام على من لا نبي بعده.

س١: ما هي الطهارة لغة وشرعا ؟

ج: الطهارة لغة النظافة وشرعا ارتفاع الحدث وزوال الخبث. ثم الحدث قسمان:

١. أكبر: وهو ما أوجب الغسل.
٢. وأصغر: وهو ما أوجب الوضوء.

س٢: كم أقسام الماء ؟ وما هي ؟

ج: أقسام الماء ثلاثة:

الأول: طهور – وهو الباقي على خلقته الأصلية، سواء نزل من السماء أو نبع من الأرض.

وهو طاهر في نفسه، مطهر لغيره. يرفع الحدث، ويزيل الخبث.

الثاني: طاهر – وهو:

١. ما تغيّر كثير من لونه أو طعمه أو ريحه بمخالطة شيء طاهر كزعفران.
٢. أو كان قليلا وأستعمل في رفع حدث. أو انغمست فيه كل يد المسلم المكلف القائم من نوم ليل قبل غسلها ثلاثا بنية وتسمية. وذلك واجب .وهو طاهر في نفسه، غير مطهر لغيره.

Chapter on Ṭahārah (purification)

Section on Water

All praise is due to Allāh alone. And peace and blessing be upon the one after whom there is no prophet.

1. What is the definition of ṭaharah linguistically and in sharīʿa?

Ṭahārah linguistically means purification (or cleanliness). In sharīʿa, it means lifting *ḥadath* (state of impurity) or removal of *khabath* (physical impurity).

As for ḥadath, it is of two types:

a. Akbar or major: that which necessitates *ghusl.*
b. Asghar or minor: that which necessitates *wuḍū.*

2. How many types of water are there? What are they?

Three types:

a. **Ṭahūr:** it is that water which remains in its original form. Whether it descended it from the sky (snow, hail etc.) or came from the ground (springs, wells, etc.). It is pure in itself, and it can purify. It lifts the ḥadath and removes khabath.

b. Ṭāhir:

   i. A large amount of water whose colour, taste and smell changes by being mixed with something pure such as saffron.
   ii. A small amount of water previously used for lifting ḥadath (e.g. used wuḍu water collected in a container) or
   iii. a religiously obligated Muslim wakes up from nocturnal sleep and dips his hand into the water before washing it three times without niyya and basmala. Doing this is wājib (can refer to niyya or basmala). This water is now pure in itself but unable to purify.

يجوز استعماله في غير رفع حدث وزوال خبث كطبخ وشرب ونحوهما .

الثالث: نجس . وهو: ما وقعت فيه نجاسة، وكان قليلا وإن لم يتغير، أو كثيرا وتغير أحد أوصافه. ولا يرفع الحدث، ولا يزيل الخبث .

والكثير: ما بلغ قلتين فأكثر .

وهما : أحد وسبعون رطلا وثلاثة أسباع رطل بالنابلسي وما وافقه .

أحكام الآنية وأجزاء الميتة

س ٣: ما الذي يُباح اتخاذه من الأواني ؟

ج: يباح اتخاذ كل إناء طاهر واستعماله، إلا آنية الذهب والفضة، فيحرم استعمالهما واتخاذهما .

س٤: ما حكم آنية الكفار وثيابهم ؟

ج: آنية الكفار وثيابهم طاهرة، ما لم تعلم نجاستها .

س٥: ما حكم أجزاء الميتة ؟

ج: عظم الميتة وقرنها نجس وكذا جلدها . ولا يطهر بالدباغ، لكن لو دبغ يباح استعماله في اليابسات دون المائعات . وأما الشعر والصوف والريش فطاهر، إن كان من حيوان طاهر في الحياة، وإن لم يكن من مأكولا كالهرة .

It is permissible to use ṭāhir water for eating and drinking etc. But not for lifting ḥadath and removal of khabath, not even for istinjā.

3. Najis: It is that water in which najāsa or filth drops and:

a. it is a small quantity (water changing is not required)
b. Or a large quantity of water where one of its three characteristics have changed (because of the filth).

This water cannot lift ḥadath nor clean khabath. A large quantity of water is: two qullas or more. (A qulla is a large container which requires a strong man to carry it. One qulla is 71 & 3/7 riṭl in Nablus or its equivalent. [3] A small quantity is anything less than the above.

Rulings of containers and parts of carrion

3. What types of containers are permissible to adopt?

It is permissible to use every pure container except those made from gold and silver. Both are ḥarām to use and adopt.

4. What is the ruling of the container and clothing of the disbelievers?

They are pure, as long as its najāsa is unknown.

5. What is the ruling on the parts of carrion?

The bones and horns are najis. So is its skin, which cannot be purified with tanning (only if the animal was slaughtered in a ḥalāl manner, it can be ṭāhir). However, if it is tanned, it is permissible to use it for dry things (e.g. storing grain), not for liquids (e.g. storing water or honey which would be impermissible nor can one pray on it). And as for hair, wool and feathers, they are pure even from **a.** carrion, **b.** pure animals while they are alive or **c.** from an animal that is not permissible to eat e.g. a cat.

---

[3] In the metric system, it is approximately 190 Litres.

أحكام الاستنجاء وآداب التخلي

س٦: ما هو الاستنجاء؟ وما حكمه؟

ج: هو إزالة ما خرج من السبيلين بماء طهور، أو حجر مباح ونحوه كالخرق.
وهو واجب لكل خارج إن لم يكن منيا، أو ريحا، أو ناشفا لم يلوث المحل كالحصى.

س٧: ما شرط صحته؟

ج: شرط صحته الإنقاء: وهو بالماء: عود خشونة المحل كما كان. وبالحجر: أن يبقى أثر لا يزيله إلا الماء. بشرط:

١. أن يمسح ثلاث مسحات تعم كل مسحة المحل.
٢. وأن لا يتجاوز الخارج موضع العادة.

والأفضل: أن يستجمر أولا بالأحجار ثم يتبعها بالماء.

س٨: ما هي آداب قاضي الحاجة؟

ج: هي:

١. أن يقدم اليسرى عند دخول الخلاء، ويقول: بسم الله، أعوذ بالله من الخبث والخبائث.
٢. وإذا خرج قدم اليمنى وقال: غفرانك، الحمد لله الذي أذهب عني الأذى وعافاني.

Rulings & etiquettes of istinjā

6. What is istinjā? What are its rulings?

It is to purify oneself from the filth of the two orifices (private parts) with pure water, or a permissible stone or the like their off e.g. rags.[4] And it is only mandatory on everything that exits the private parts as long as it is not semen, wind or dry excretion resembling a pebble (in dryness and hardness) and does not pollute the surrounding area.

7. What is the prerequisite of a sound istinjā?

The prerequisite is cleanliness with water until the area returns to its original state as it was before it became filthy. And if it is with a stone, there does not remains any filth except that which can only be removed with water. Wiping with stones have the following conditions:

a. Wipe three times the area that requires purity
b. excretion does not exceed beyond the normal area the filth usually touches.

Best way to do istinjā is to use a stone first and then use water.

8. What are the etiquettes of one who relieves himself?

They are to enter with the left foot into the lavatory, and say: بِسْمِ اللهِ أَعُوْذُ بِاللهِ مِنَ الْخُبُثِ وَالْخَبَآئِثِ *In the name of Allāh, I seek refuge from the male and female jinns.* And to exit with the right foot and say: غُفْرَانَكَ اَلْحَمْدُ لِلّٰهِ الَّذِيْ أَذْهَبَ عَنِّي الْأَذٰى وَعَافَانِيْ *Your forgiveness, all praises are due to Allāh who removed from me discomfort and blessed me with relief.*

---

[4] Today, the equivalent would be toilet paper.

س٩: ما يكره لقاضي الحاجة؟ وما يحرم عليه؟

ج: يكره له:

١. استقبال الشمس والقمر.

٢. ومهب الريح.

٣. والكلام.

٤. والبول في إناء بلا حاجة.

٥. وفي شق.

٦. ونار.

٧. ورماد.

ويحرم عليه:

١. استقبال القبلة، واستدبارها في الصحراء بلا حائل.

٢. وأن يقضي حاجته في طريق مسلوك.

٣. أو ظل نافع.

٤. وتحت شجرة مثمرة.

٥. وأن يلبث فوق حاجته.

ويجوز البول قائما إذا أمن ناظرا أو تلويثا .

9. What is *makrūh* & *ḥarām* for one relieving himself?

It is makrūh to:

a. face the sun or moon
b. face into the wind
c. speaking
d. urinating in a container without necessity
e. urinating in a crack in the ground.[5]
f. into a fire
g. into ashes

And it is ḥarām to:

a. to face or have back to the qibla in the open-air without a barrier
b. to relieve oneself on a path
c. or beneficial shade
d. or under a fruit-bearing tree
e. to remain (in the lavatory) more than needed

It is permissible to urinate standing if one will not be exposed to anybody or will not dirty oneself.

[5] There could be animals, insects or snakes.

أحكام السواك

س١٠: ما حكم السواك؟ وفي أي محل يتأكد ؟ وما فائدته؟

ج: السواك مسنون كل وقت، لغير صائم بعد الزوال فيكره. ويتأكد :

١. عند وضوء
٢. وصلاة
٣. وقراءة قرآن
٤. وانتباه من نوم
٥. وتغير رائحة فم
٦. ودخول مسجد
٧. ومنزل
٨. وإطالة سكوت
٩. وصفرة أسنان
١٠. وخلو معدة من طعام

وفوائده كثيرة، منها :

١. أنه يهضم الطعام
٢. ويشد لحمة الأسنان.
٣. وأعظمها : أنه يذكر الشهادة عند الموت.

Rulings of Siwāk

10. What is the ruling of siwāk (using a tooth stick) and when is it emphasised what are its benefits?

Siwāk is sunna at all times, however it is makrūh for the fasting person after zenith.

It is emphasised:

a. at the time of wuḍū
b. (before) ṣalāt
c. (before) reading Qurān
d. (after) waking from sleep
e. (after) change of mouth odour (bad breath)
f. (before) entering the Masjid
g. (before) entering the home
h. (after) prolonged silence
i. at the yellowing of the teeth
j. (after) having an empty stomach.

Its benefits are many, such as:

a. It helps with digestion of food
b. strengthens the gums
c. The greatest is that it will aid in reminding of the Shahāda at the time of death.

س١١: ما الذي يسن فعله من التنظيف وتحسين الهيئة؟

ج: يسن:

١. حلق العانة.

٢. ونتف الإبط.

٣. وقص الأظافر.

٤. والنظر في المرآة.

٥. والاكتحال كل ليلة.

٦. وحف الشارب.

٧. وإعفاء اللحية.

وحرم حلقها، ولا بأس بأخذ ما زاد على القبضة منها.

أحكام الوضوء

س١٢: كم فرائض الوضوء؟ وما هي:

ج: فروض الوضوء ستة، وهي:

١. غسل الوجه، ومنه: المضمضة والاستنشاق.

٢. وغسل اليدين مع المرفقين، والمرفق: هو العظم الفاصل بين الدراع والعضد.

٣. ومسح جميع ظاهر الرأس، ومنه الأذنان: والبياض الذي فوقهما.

٤. وغسل الرجلين مع الكعبين، وهما: العظمان الناتئان في أسفل الساق.

11. What are the sunna actions of cleanliness and personal grooming?

It is sunna to:

a. shave the pubic region (trimming or using chemicals are also sunna)
b. pluck the armpit hairs
c. clip the nails (finger and toes)
d. utilise a mirror
e. use ithmid (antimony) every night
f. trim the moustache (including the sides) very short.
g. lengthen the beard

It is haram to shave the beard, but it is permissible (but not ideal) to trim that which exceeds a fist length.

Rulings of Wuḍū

12. How many farḍ actions (pl. farāiḍ or obligatory actions) are there in wuḍū and what are they?

There are six farḍ actions in wuḍū and they are:

a. Washing the face which includes rinsing the mouth and nose.
b. Washing both hands up to and including the elbow. The elbow is a protruding bone (joint) that connects the upper-arm & forearm.
c. Wipe the outside of the entire head which also includes both ears and the area above and around the top of the ear (where hair does not grow).
d. And washing both feet up to and including the ankles. The ankles are the two bones protruding at the bottom of the (side of the) shin.

٥. والترتيب بين الأعضاء .
٦. والمولاة، وهي: أن لا يؤخر غسل عضو إلى أن يجف ما قبله بزمن معتدل .

س١٣: ما الذي يجب في الوضوء ؟

ج: يجب فيه التسمية فقط . وتسقط بتركها سهوا، أو جهلا لا عمدا .

س١٤: كم شروط الوضوء ؟

ج: شروطه ثمانية، وهي:

١. انقطاع ما يوجبه من بول وريح وحيض ونفاس ونحو ذلك .
٢. والنية .
٣. والإسلام .
٤. والعقل .
٥. والتمييز أي بلوغ سبع سنين .
٦. والماء الطهور المباح .
٧. وإزالة ما يمنع وصول الماء من شمع أو عجين أو نحوهما .
٨. والاستنجاء أو الاستجمار .

e. Maintain the order from one limb to another.
f. To do so without long interruption i.e. to not delay for a considerable time in the washing of a limb so that the previous limb dries.

13. What is wājib (necessary) in wuḍū?

Only tasmiya (saying of *bismillāh)* is wājib.

It is excused, if it is left out forgetfully or in ignorance, but not so if it is left out intentionally.

14. How many prerequisites does wuḍū have?

It has eight prerequisites, which are:

a. ceasing of that which necessitates wuḍū such as urination, passing wind, menses and the like thereof.
b. intention
c. to be Muslim
d. sound of mind
e. reaching the age of discretion which is reaching 7 years of age.
f. pure water acquired legally
g. the removal of anything which prevents water reaching the body such as wax or dough or anything that resembles it.
h. Istinjā (cleaning the private parts with water) or istijmār (cleaning with stone or something dry, such as toilet paper).

س١٥: كم سنن الوضوء ؟ وما هي ؟

ج: سننه ثمانية عشر، وهي:

١. استقبال القبلة.
٢. والسواك.
٣. وغسل الكفين ثلاثا، لغير قائم من نوم ليل، فيجب بنية وتسمية كما تقدم.
٤. والبداءة بالمضمضة والاستنشاق قبل غسل الوجه.
٥. والمبالغة فيهما لغير الصائم.
٦. والمبالغة في سائر الأعضاء.
٧. والزيادة في ماء الوجه.
٨. وتخليل اللحية الكثيفة.
٩. وتخليل أصابع اليدين والرجلين.
١٠. وأخذ ماء جديد للأذنين.
١١. وتقديم اليمنى على اليسرى من اليدين والرجلين.
١٢. ومجاوزة محل الفرض في الأعضاء الأربعة.
١٣. والغسلة الثانية والثالثة.
١٤. واستصحاب النية إلى آخر الوضوء.
١٥. والإتيان بالنية عند غسل الكفين.

15. How many sunnas are there in wuḍū?

It has eighteen sunnas[6] and they are:

a. facing the Qibla

b. using the miswāk

c. washing the hands three times. However, for those who wake up from a nocturnal sleep then doing so is wājib with intention and saying *basmala* - as has been already mentioned

d. rinsing the mouth and nose before washing the face

e. to do more than the required for both the mouth and nose except for the fasting person (i.e. except for the fasting person, water should go high in the nose and completely to the back of the mouth)

f. to be thorough in cleaning all the limbs

g. increase in water for the face (as there are wrinkles, crevices, and beard on the face)

h. combing a thick beard (with wet fingers) once

i. running wet fingers between the fingers and toes

j. taking new water for the ears

k. right limb to precede the left for hands and feet

l. to exceed the beyond the farḍ area for the four farḍ limbs

m. to wash a second and third time

n. keep the intention until the end of wuḍū

o. make the intention when washing the hands

[6] The author has mentioned eighteen but listed nineteen. Number eighteen is the additional point and is not considered by most Ḥanbali imāms.

١٦. والنطق بها سرا .

١٧. وقول ما ورد بعد فراغه وهو أشهد أن لا إله إلا الله وحده لا شريك له، وأشهد أن محمدا عبده ورسوله، اللهم اجعلني من التوابين، واجعلني من عبادك المتطهرين، مع رفع بصره إلى السماء ،

١٨. وقراءة سورة القدر .

١٩. وأن يتولى وضوؤه بنفسه .

س١٦: أخبرني عن صفة الوضوء الكامل ؟

ج: صفته:

١. أن ينوي الوضوء للصلاة .

٢. ثم يقول: بسم الله .

٣. ويغسل كفيه ثلاثا .

٤. ثم يتمضمض، ويستنشق ثلاثا ثلاثا .

٥. ثم يغسل وجهه ثلاثا من منبت شعر الرأس المعتاد إلى منتهى الذقن طولا، ومن الأذن إلى الأذن عرضا .

٦. ثم يغسل يديه مع مرفقيه ثلاثا .

٧. ثم يمسح جميع ظاهر رأسه، يمر يديه من مقدمه إلى قفاه، ويعيدهما .

٨. ويدخل سبابتيه في صماخ أذنيه، ويمسح بإبهاميه ظاهرهما .

٩. ثم يغسل رجليه مع كعبيه ثلاثا .

p. to pronounce (the intention) silently.[7]
q. And to say the following du'ā while raising the gaze to the sky after wuḍū:

أَشْهَدُ أَنْ لا إِلٰهَ إِلَّا اللّٰهُ وَحْدَهُ لا شَرِيكَ لَهُ وَأَشْهَدُ أَنَّ مُحَمَّداً عَبْدُهُ وَرَسُولُهُ اللَّهُمَّ اجْعَلْنِي مِنَ التَّوَّابِينَ وَاجْعَلْنِي مِنْ عِبَادِكَ الْمُتَطَهِّرِينَ

I bear witness that there is no one worthy of worship except Allāh alone who has no partner. I bear witness that Muḥammad is his slave and messenger. O Allāh make me from the repentant and those of your slaves who are purified.

r. to recite Surah Qadr

s. To do the wuḍū without assistance.

16. Inform me about the complete description of wuḍū.

Its description is:

a. to make intention for wuḍū of ṣalāt
b. then say Bismillāh
c. wash hands three times
d. rinse the mouth and nose three times each
e. wash the face three times from the top of the forehead to the bottom of the chin and ear to ear
f. wash the arms up to and including the elbow three times
g. wipe the whole head passing wet hands from the front of the hairline to the nape and wipe them back from the nape to the front.
h. to insert the index fingers in the ears, and wipe the back of the ears with the thumbs
i. to wash the feet up to and including the ankles three times

[7] There is a difference of opinion of this being sunna. The research scholars have pointed out that there is no ḥadīth text establishing it as a sunna.

أحكام المسح على الخفين

س١٧: ما حكم المسح على الخفين؟

ج: يجوز بشروط سبعة، وهي:

١. لبسهما بعد كمال الطهارة بالماء.

٢. وسترهما لمحل الفرض.

٣. وإمكان المشي بهما عرفا.

٤. وثبوتهما بنفسهما.

٥. وإباحتهما.

٦. وطهارة عينهما.

٧. وعدم وصفهما البشرة.

س١٨: كم مدة المسح عليهما؟ وما المقدار الذي يجب مسحه؟

ج: يمسح مقيم وعاص بسفره يوما وليلة من حين حدث بعد لبس.

ويمسح مسافر سفر قصر، ثلاثة أيام بلياليها، ومسافة القصر: يومان معتدلان بسير الأثقال ودبيب الأقدام.

ويجب مسح أكثر أعلاه، ولا يجزئ مسح أسفله ولا عقبه، ولا يسن ذلك.

Rulings of masaḥ (wiping) on khuffs

17. What is the ruling of masaḥ on khuffs (leather socks)?

It is permissible with seven prerequisites, and they are:

a. to wear them after complete purification with water (that is after wuḍū).
b. they cover the area of the foot that needs to be washed (including the ankles)
c. the possibility to walk around in them
d. they remain on the feet by themselves
e. it is permissible to use (not stolen, or usurped, or made from silk for men)
f. leather that is pure (slaughtered/hunted islamically)
g. cannot see skin through them

18. How long will the masaḥ last? What is the wājib area of the masaḥ?

It is permissible for the resident and the sinful (traveller intending evil) to wipe for a day and a night (24 hours) from the time that he breaks his wuḍū after wearing them (i.e. 24 hours start after breaking wuḍū).

It is permissible for the traveller of a journey in which one can shorten prayers to wipe for three days and nights (72 hours).

And the distance of shortening is: two moderate days with light luggage and walking (approximately 80 kms).

It is wājib to wipe most of the upper portion of the khuff. The bottom of the foot and heel does not take the place of the top and nor is it sunna.

س١٩: ما يبطل المسح عليهما ؟

ج: يبطله أحد ثلاثة أشياء وهي:

١. ما أوجب الغسل.

٢. أو ظهور بعض محل الفرض.

٣. أو انقضاء مدة المسح.

س٢٠: هل يجوز المسح على غير الخفين ؟

ج: نعم، يجوز المسح على الجبيرة، وهي: أخشاب أو خرق تربط على الكسر أو الجرح.

س٢١: أخبرني عن حكم المسح عليها ؟

ج: إن وضعها على طهارة، ولم تتجاوز محل الحاجة، غسل الصحيح، ومسح على الجريح.

وإن تجاوزت وخيف الضرر بنزعها، وجب مع المسح التيمم للزائد.

وإن وضعها على غير طهارة غسل الصحيح، وتيمم بلا مسح تجاوزت أم لا.

باب نواقض الوضوء

س٢٢: كم نواقض الوضوء ؟

ج: نواقض الوضوء ثمانية، وهي:

١. الخارج من السبيلين قليلا كان أو كثيرا، طاهرا أو نجسا.

19. What annuls the wiping on the khuffs?

Three things invalidate the wiping:

a. that which necessities ghusl
b. or some of the area that the khuff should cover (i.e. the feet and ankles) becomes exposed
c. or the end of the period of wiping

20. Is it permissible to wipe on other than khuffs?

Yes, it is permissible to wipe on a jabīra (splint) which is wood, rags or bandages that are tied to a bone fracture or a wound.

21. Inform me what is the ruling on wiping on them?

a. If it is applied while in the state of tahāra, and:
   i. it does not go beyond the place of necessity, he washes everything and wipes on the wound.
   ii. it goes beyond the actual wound and there is harm in taking it off, it is wājib to make tayammum with the wiping.
b. If he placed it without the state of tahāra, then he washes everything else and he makes tayammum without wiping whether he exceeds beyond the wound or not.

Section on the invalidators of wuḍū

22. How many invalidators of wuḍū are there?

There are eight invalidators of wuḍū:

a. what exits from the two orifices (urethra and anus) whether little or a lot, ṭāhir or najis.

٢. وخروج النجاسة من بقية البدن، فإن كان الخارج بولا أو غائطا نقض مطلقا وإن كان غيرهما كالدم والقيء، نقض إن كثر عند كل أحد بحسب نفسه.

٣. وزوال العقل بجنون، أو تغطيته بنحو نوم، ما لم يكن يسيرا عرفا من جالس متمكن أو قائم.

٤. ومس فرج الآدمي قبلا أو دبرا باليد بلا حائل.

٥. ولمس الذكر بشرة الأنثى، والأنثى بشرة الذكر بشهوة، ولو كان الملموس ميتا أو عجوزا أو محرما.

٦. وغسل الميت أو بعضه.

٧. وأكل لحم الإبل ولو نيئا.

٨. والردة عن الإسلام والعياذ بالله تعالى.

وكل ما أوجب الغسل أوجب الوضوء إلا الموت.

س٢٣: ما حكم من شك في الطهارة؟

ج: من تيقن الطهارة وشك في الحدث، أو تيقن الحدث وشك في الطهارة، عمل بما تيقن.

س٢٤: ما يحرم على المحدث فعله؟

ج: يحرم على المحدث حدث أصغر أو أكبر:

١. الصلاة.

٢. والطواف

b. najāsa exits from the rest of the body. If what exits is urine or stool then wuḍū will always break, as for what is other than these two e.g. blood/pus & vomit then it breaks if it is a lot according to the estimation of the person himself

c. losing one's senses through insanity or intellect is suspended e.g. sleep or the like thereof, which is generally not considered if it is a short sleep when firmly seated or sleeping while standing

d. touching the private parts of a human whether the penis/vagina or the anus with the hand without a barrier

e. touching the skin of the opposite gender with lust whether the one touched is dead, old or a maḥram

f. washing a corpse or some of it

g. eating of the camel meat (not organs or its soup) even if it is raw

h. becoming an apostate from Islām - May Allāh protect us and with Allāh is safety

Everything that necessities ghusl necessities wuḍū except death.

23. What is the ruling of one who doubts his tahāra?

Whoever is certain of his state of purity but doubts his impurity or is certain of his impurity and doubts his purity then he should act on what he is certain.

24. What is forbidden for one in a state of impurity?

It is forbidden for the one in the state of impurity whether it is major or minor:

a. ṣalāt

b. ṭawāf of the Ka'bā

٣. ومس المصحف بلا حائل.

وعلى المحدث حدث أكبر:

١. قراءة القرآن.

٢. والجلوس في المسجد بلا وضوء.

باب الغسل

س٢٥: كم موجبات الغسل؟ وما هي؟

ج: موجبات الغسل سبعة، وهي:

١. انتقال المني من مقره.

٢. وخروجه من مخرجه المعتاد بلذة، فإن خرج لغير ذلك لم يوجب الغسل.

٣. وتغييب الحشفة، أو قدرها من مقطوعها بلا حائل، في فرج أصلي ولو دبرا، أو لميت، أو بهيمة، أو طائر.

٤. وإسلام الكافر، ولو مرتدا.

٥. والحيض.

٦. والنفاس.

٧. والموت، تعبدا.

c. Touching a muṣḥaf (Qurān) without a barrier

And as for the one in the major state of impurity, it is forbidden to:

a. recite the Qurān (from memory, even if it is a verse or more. However, the Basmala or any duʿās which appear in the Qurān may be recited with the intention of duʿā)
b. staying inside a masjid without wuḍū (so if a person in major impurity performs wuḍū, he may stay in the masjid)

Section on ghusl (bathing)

25. How many things necessitate ghusl and what are they?

Seven things necessitate ghusl and they are:

a. Semen moving from its point of origin (whether it flows out of the urethra or not)
b. semen exiting from the penis with desire; if it exits without desire, it does not necessitate ghusl
c. penetration of the full penis or part of the head without a barrier, whether it be vaginal or anal, whether it be with a dead human or animal (this can occur for someone under duress)
d. when a disbeliever becomes a Muslim even if he was murtad
e. end of menses
f. end of post-natal bleeding
g. death, as an act of worship (it is not due to the body of the deceased becoming dirty as opposed to the first six)

س٢٦: كم شروط الغسل؟ وما هي؟

ج: شروط الغسل سبعة، وهي:

١. انقطاع ما يوجبه.
٢. والنية.
٣. والإسلام.
٤. والعقل.
٥. والتمييز.
٦. والماء الطهور المباح.
٧. وإزالة ما يمنع وصول الماء إلى الجسد.

س٢٧: ما الذي يجب في الغسل؟

ج: يجب فيه شيء واحد، وهو التسمية. وتسقط سهوا وجهلا، لا عمدا.

س٢٨: ما فرض الغسل؟

ج: فرضه شيء واحد، وهو: أن يعم بالماء جميع بدنه، وداخل فمه وأنفه.

س٢٩: كم سنن الغسل؟ وما هي؟

ج: سننه سبعة، وهي:

26. How many prerequisites of ghusl are there? And what are they?

There are seven prerequisites of ghusl and they are:

a. ending of what made it wājib

b. intention

c. being Muslim

d. being of sound intellect

e. being discerning (sound reasoning that distinguishes between right and wrong)

f. ṭahūr water that is acquired in a ḥalāl manner

g. removal of what prevents water reaching the body (e.g. paint, wax, etc...)

27. What is wājib in ghusl?

There is only one wājib in ghusl i.e. saying bismillah. If one omits it out of forgetfulness or ignorance than it does not invalidate the ghusl. However, if it is omitted intentionally then ghusl is invalid.

28. What is the farḍ of ghusl?

There is only one farḍ of ghusl which is to wash the whole body including the inside of the mouth & nose.

29. How many sunnas of ghusl are there and what are they?

There are seven sunnas of ghusl and they are:

1. الوضوء قبله.
2. وإزالة ما على الفرج والبدن من مني ونجاسة.
3. وإفراغ الماء على رأسه ثلاثا، وعلى بقية بدنه ثلاثا.
4. والتيامن.
5. والموالاة.
6. وإمرار اليد على الجسد.
7. وإعادة غسل رجليه بمكان آخر.

س ٣٠: كم الأغسال المسنونات؟ وما هي؟

ج: الأغسال المسنونات ستة عشر، وهي:

1. الغسل لصلاة جمعة في يومها، لذكر حضرها.
2. والغسل لأجل غسل ميت.
3. ولصلاة عيد في يومه.
4. ولصلاة كسوف.
5. واستسقاء.
6. ولجنون.
7. وإغماء.
8. والاستحاضة لكل صلاة.

a. to do wuḍū before it
b. to remove from the private parts and the body semen or filth
c. to pour water on the head three times, and on the rest of the body three times
d. to do so starting with the right
e. continuity (to not give a long gap between the washing of each limb)
f. rubbing with the hand all over the body
g. washing the feet again in another location

30. How many sunna ghusls are there? What are they?

There are sixteen types of sunna ghusls and they are:

a. for the jumuʿa prayer in its day for a male resident (non-traveller)
b. giving ghusl to the dead
c. the ʿīd prayer on its day
d. the eclipse prayer
e. the rain prayer
f. due to madness
g. after fainting
h. during chronic bleeding before every ṣalāt

٩. والإحرام.
١٠. ولدخول مكة ولو مع حيض.
١١. ولدخول حرمها.
١٢. ولوقوف بعرفة.
١٣. ولطواف زيارة.
١٤. ولطواف وداع.
١٥. ولمبيت بمزدلفة.
١٦. ولرمي جمار.

ويتيمم للكل استحبابا للحاجة.

باب التيمم

س٣١: كم شروط صحة التيمم؟ وما هي؟

ج: شروط صحة التيمم ثمانية، وهي:

١. النية.
٢. والإسلام.
٣. والعقل.
٤. والتمييز.

i. for iḥrām
j. entering city of Makkah, even if in menses
k. entering the sanctuary around Makkah
l. before standing at ʿArafāt
m. before ṭawāf al ziyāra
n. before ṭawāf al widāʿ (farewell ṭawāf)
o. staying the night at Muzdalifa
p. before stoning of the Jamarāt

And to make tayyamum is mustaḥab for all the above out of necessity [8]

Section on Tayammum

31. How many prerequisites are there for the validity of tayammum? What are they?

Prerequisites for the validity of tayammum are eight, and they are:

a. intention
b. Islām
c. sound intellect
d. age of discernment

---

[8] as a replacement for ghusl whenever one is unable to do ghusl (due to sickness, cold, water being too expensive or unavailable etc.)

٥. والاستنجاء أو الاستجمار .

٦. دخول وقت الصلاة المتيمم لها .

٧. وعدم القدرة على استعمال الماء .

٨. وأن يكون:

١. بتراب .

٢. مباح.

٣. غير مستعمل .

٤. ولا محترق

٥. له غبار يعلق باليد .

س٣٢: ما واجب التيمم؟

ج: يجب فيه التسمية . وتسقط سهوا وجهلا، لا عمدا .

س٣٣: كم فروض التيمم؟ وما هي؟

ج: فروضه خمسة، وهي:

١. مسح الوجه دون الفم .

٢. ومسح اليدين إلى الكوعين .

٣. والترتيب .

e. istinjā or istijmār (dry cleaning of private parts).
f. entering of the time of ṣalāt for which tayyamum is being made
g. inability to use water
h. to be:
    i. soil, dirt, dust
    ii. permissible (i.e. acquired lawfully)
    iii. not be pre-used
    iv. not burnt
    v. it has dust that attaches to the hand (when touched)

32. What is wājib for tayammum?

It is wājib to say bismillah. It is excused if one omits it out of forgetfulness or ignorance, but not intentionally.

33. How many farḍs are there for tayammum? What are they?

There are five farḍs, they are:

a. to wipe the face other than the mouth
b. wiping the hands up to the wrists
c. maintain the correct order

٤. والموالاة في الطهارة الصغرى.

٥. وتعيين النية لما يتيمم له، من حدث أصغر، أو أكبر، أو من نجاسة على البدن.

س ٣٤: كم مبطلات التيمم؟ وما هي؟

ج: مبطلاته خمسة، وهي:

١. ما أبطل الوضوء.

٢. ووجود الماء.

٣. وخروج الوقت.

٤. وزوال العذر المبيح.

٥. وخلع نحو الخف إن تيمم وهو لابسه.

فصل في إزالة النجاسة

س٣٥: كيف يطهر المتنجس؟

ج: إذا كانت النجاسة من الكلب والخنزير وما تولد منهما أو من أحدهما يغسل المتنجس سبع مرات إحداهن بتراب طهور. وإن كانت من غير ذلك، يغسل سبعا بالماء فقط. ويكفي في بول صبي لم يأكل الطعام نضحه وغمره بالماء. وتطهر أرض ونحوها بإزالة عين النجاسة بالماء

d. to maintain continuity for tayammum done for the minor state of impurity.

e. to specify intention for what tayammum is made for, whether for minor or major states of impurity, or removal of najāsa on the body.

34. How many invalidators does tayammum have and what are they?

There are five invalidators of tayammum:

a. whatever invalidates wuḍū

b. finding water

c. exiting of the time (tayammum only lasts for one ṣalāt time)

d. ending of the cause of tayammum

e. removal of a khuff, if tayammum was made while wearing it.

Section on removal of impurities

35. How does one purify something that has become filthy?

If the impurity is from a dog or a pig, or what is born from either of them or from one of them[9]. It should be washed seven times and one of which is with dirt (or soap). If the impurity is other than a dog or a pig it is washed seven times with water only.

It is sufficient for the urine of a boy (less than two) who has not eaten food (breast fed only) to drench it by sprinkling water from the hand. And the ground is purified and that which is similar to it (other surfaces) are purified by the removal of actual impurity with water.

---

[9] Can refer to cross species breeding with a dog or pig. Genetic modification has made this somewhat possible today.

س ٣٦: ما الطاهر وما النجس من الحيوان؟

ج: ما لا يؤكل لحمه من الطير والبهائم مما فوق الهرة نجس. وما دونها كالفأرة طاهر. وكل ميتة نجسة إلا:

١. ميتة الآدمي.

٢. والسمك.

٣. والجراد.

٤. وما لا دم له سائل، كالعقرب.

س٣٧: ما حكم الخارج مما يؤكل لحمه؟

ج: ما أكل لحمه: فبوله وروثه، وكل خارج منه طاهر، إلا الدم والقيح، لكن يعفى عن يسيره في الصلاة.

س٣٨: ما حكم الخارج مما لا يؤكل لحمه؟

ج: كل خارج منه نجس، إلا مني الآدمي ولبنه فطاهر. ويعفى في الصلاة عن يسير الدّم والقيح منه، إن كان طاهرا في الحياة.

باب الحيض والنفاس

س٣٩: ما هو الحيض؟

ج: هو دم طبيعة وجبلة، يخرج من المرأة مع الصحة من غير سبب ولادة في أوقات معلومة. ولا حيض قبل تسع. ولا بعد خمسين سنة. ولا مع حمل.

36. What is ṭāhir and what is najis from animals?

Animals and birds bigger in size than a cat and whose flesh cannot be eaten are najis. What is smaller such as a mouse is ṭāhir.

Every carrion is impure except for

a. a human being.
b. fish
c. locusts
d. that which does not have flowing blood like a scorpion.

37. What is the ruling of that which exits from an islamically edible animal?

The urine and faeces of islamically edible animals and everything that exits from is ṭāhir except for blood and pus. However, a small amount of it is excused in ṣalāt.

38. What is the ruling for that which exits an islamically non-edible animal?

Everything that exits from it, is najis or impure except for human semen and milk.

In ṣalāt a small amount of blood and pus (from non-edible animals and humans but not pigs) if the animal is ṭāhir when it is alive are excused.

Section on Ḥayḍ and Nifās

39. What is Ḥayḍ (menses)?

It is natural bleeding that exits from a healthy woman other than birth. It is at specific intervals. There is no ḥayḍ before the age of nine nor after the age of fifty. It cannot occur during pregnancy.

س٤٠ : كم أقل مدة الحيض؟ وما أكثرها ؟ وما غالبها ؟

ج: أقلها يوم وليلة. وأكثرها خمسة عشر يوما . وغالبها ست أو سبع.

س٤١: كم أقل الطهر بين الحيضتين؟

ج: أقله ثلاثة عشر يوما . وغالبه بقية الشهر. ولا حد لأكثره.

س٤٢: ما هو النفاس؟ وما أكثره؟ وما أقله؟

ج: هو دم يخرج مع الولادة أو قبلها بيومين أو ثلاثة. وأكثره أربعون يوما . ولا حد لأقله.

س٤٣: ما يحرم بالحيض والنفاس؟

ج: يحرم أشياء، منها:

١. الوطء.

٢. والصلاة.

٣. والصوم.

٤. والطواف.

٥. وقراءة القرآن.

٦. ومس المصحف.

٧. والجلوس في المسجد.

ومتى طهرت يجب عليها قضاء الصوم لا الصلاة.

40. What is the minimum, maximum and general length of time of ḥayḍ?

The minimum is a day and a night. The maximum is fifteen days. Generally, it is six or seven days.

41. What is the least tuhr (state of purity) between two ḥayḍs?

The minimum tuhr is thirteen days. Generally, it is the rest of the month (29 or 30 days). There is no maximum limit for tuhr.

42. What is nifās? What is its maximum and minimum length of time?

It is blood that comes out after birth or two or three days before birth. It is a maximum of forty days and there is no minimum limit for it.

43. What is ḥarām in ḥayḍ and nifās?

During ḥayḍ and nifās it is ḥarām:

a. to have intercourse
b. pray ṣalāt
c. fast
d. do ṭawāf
e. recite Qurān
f. touch a musḥaf
g. remain in a masjid

When the woman is purified from these states, she must make up the missed fasts but not the ṣalāt.

كتاب الصلاة

س٤٤: ما حكم الأذان والإقامة؟

ج: حكم الأذان والإقامة أنهما فرضا كفاية في الحضر على الرجال الأحرار. ويسنان للمنفرد، وفي السفر. ويكرهان للنساء، ولو بلا رفع صوت. ولا يصحان إلا:

١. مرتبين.
٢. متواليين عرفا.
٣. وأن يكونا من واحد، بنية منه. أي: لو أذن واحد بعض الأذان أو الإقامة، وأتمهما آخر لم يصحا.

س٤٥: ما يشترط في المؤذن؟

ج: يشترط في المؤذن ستة شروط:

١. كونه مسلما.
٢. ذكرا.
٣. عاقلا.
٤. مميزا.
٥. ناطقا.
٦. عدلا ولو ظاهرا.

Chapter on Ṣalāt

Section on Athān

44. What is the ruling of athān and iqāma?

The ruling of athān and iqāma is that they are farḍ kifāya (communally obligatory) on free men who are not travelling.

It is sunna for an individual and those travelling.

It is makrūh for women, even if it is without raising the voice.

It would not be correct unless done:

a. in order
b. and with continuity as normally understood
c. athān or iqāma to be done by one person completely with an intention from him. It would not be correct if some of the athān or iqāma is done by one person and then completed by another.

45. What are the prerequisites of a mu'aththin?

The mu'aththin must have six prerequisites and they are to be:

a. a Muslim
b. a male
c. of sound intellect
d. discerning
e. able to speak
f. upright (islamically) if even it is external

س٤٦: هل يصح الأذان والإقامة قبل الوقت أم لا؟

ج: لا يصحان قبل الوقت، إلا أذان الفجر، فيصح بعد نصف الليل.

س٤٧: ما ركن الأذان؟

ج: ركنه: رفع الصوت به، ما لم يؤذن لحاضر.

ويسن كون المؤذن:

١. صيتا.
٢. أمينا.
٣. عالما بالوقت.
٤. متطهرا.
٥. قائما فيهما.

س٤٨: ما يسن لمن سمع المؤذن أو المقيم؟

ج: يسن للمؤذن، ولمن سمعه، أو سمع المقيم أن يقول مثله. إلا في الحيعلة، فيقول: لا حول ولا قوة إلا بالله.

46. Is athān or iqāma acceptable before its time or not?

Neither is acceptable before it's time except for the athān of Fajr. It can be done after midnight.

47. What are the arkān (plural of rukn or compulsory pillars) of athān?

Its arkān are to raise one's voice. As long as it is not done for those who are present only.[10]

It is sunna for the mu'aththin to:

a. have a loud voice
b. be trustworthy
c. knowledgeable of the (ṣalāt) time
d. be pure (i.e. be in as state of wuḍū)
e. be standing for both (i.e. for athān and iqāma)

48. What is the sunna for the one who hears the mu'aththin or muqīm (one giving iqāma, also called mukabbir)?

It is sunna for the mu'aththin and the one who hears him or hears the muqīm to repeat the same. Except when he says the Ḥay'ala[11], then the reply should be لَا حَوْلَ وَلَا قُوَّةَ إِلَّا بِاللهِ. *There is no might or strength except with Allāh.*

---

[10] Meaning that the mu'aththin is raising his voice to call people at a distance. He doesn't need to raise his voice for those present, if they are the only ones praying. However, if he raises his voice it is better.

[11] Saying of حَيَّ عَلى الصَّلَاة and حَيَّ عَلى الْفَلَاح i.e. *Hasten to salāt* and *Hasten to success.*

وإلا في التثويب، وهو قول المؤذن في أذان الفجر: الصلاة خير من النوم، فيقول سامعه: صدقت وبررت. ويقول عند لفظ الإقامة: أقامها الله وأدامها. ويصلي على النبي صلى الله عليه وسلم إذا فرغ، ويقول: اللهم رب هذه الدعوة التامة، والصلاة القائمة، آت محمدا الوسيلة والفضيلة، وابعثه مقاما محمودا الذي وعدته. ثم يدعو هنا، وعند الإقامة.

س٤٩: هل يحرم الخروج من المسجد بعد الأذان أم لا؟

ج: يحرم الخروج من المسجد بعد الأذان بلا عذر أو نية رجوع.

باب حكم الصلاة

س٥٠: على من تجب الصلاة؟

ج: تجب الصلاة على كل:

١. مسلم.
٢. مكلف.
٣. غير حائض ونفساء.

ولا تسقط عن الإنسان ما دام عقله باقيا. وتصح من مميز، والثواب له. ويلزم وليه أن يأمره بها لسبع سنين، ويضربه عليها إذا بلغ عشر سنين. ومن تركها منكرا لوجوبها فقد كفر.

However, after the tathwīb which is when the mu'aththin during the Fajr athān says اَلصَّلَاةُ خَيْرٌ مِنَ النَّوْمِ *Prayer is better than sleep*, one should reply with صَدَقْتَ وَبَرَرْتَ *You spoke the truth and you have done good.* After the words of iqāma, the reply should be أَقَامَهَا اللهُ وَأَدَامَهَا *May Allāh establish it and make it endure.*
After the athān, ṣalawāt on the Prophet ﷺ and the following du'ā should be recited: اَللَّهُمَّ رَبَّ هَذِهِ الدَّعْوَةِ التَّامَّةِ، وَالصَّلَاةِ الْقَائِمَةِ، آتِ مُحَمَّدًا الْوَسِيْلَةَ وَالْفَضِيْلَةَ، وَابْعَثْهُ مَقَامًا مَّحْمُوْدًا الَّذِيْ وَعَدتَّهُ *O Allāh! Lord of this complete call and established prayer give Muḥammad the position and distinction, and bestow upon him the praised station which you have promised.* Then other du'ās can be made and also du'ā can be made at iqāma.

49. Is it ḥarām to leave the masjid after the athān or not?

Once the athān is called, it is ḥarām to leave the masjid without an excuse or intention of returning.

Section on the ruling of ṣalāt

50. Upon whom is ṣalāt wājib?

Ṣalāt is wājib on every islamically-obligated Muslim who is not in the state of ḥayḍ or nifās. As long as the person remains sane, the obligation of ṣalāt will also remain.

Ṣalāt is correct for a person that has reached the age of discernment and he will have a reward for it. It is the duty of the guardian to order him at the age of seven and hit him at the age of ten for non-performance (ten means the completion of the tenth lunar year).

Whoever abandons ṣalāt denying it being wājib becomes kāfir.

باب مواقيت الصلاة

س٥١: ما أوقات الصلاة؟

ج: وقت الظهر: من زوال الشمس إلى أن يصير ظل كل شيء مثله سوى ظل الزوال.

ثم يليه الوقت المختار للعصر حتى يصير ظل كل شيء مثليه سوى ظل الزوال. ثم هو وقت ضرورة يحرم تأخير الصلاة إليه إلى غروب الشمس.

ووقت المغرب: من غروب الشمس إلى أن يغيب الشفق الأحمر.

ووقت العشاء المختار: من مغيب الشفق الأحمر إلى ثلث الليل الأول. ثم هو وقت ضرورة إلى طلوع الفجر.

ووقت الصبح: من طلوع الفجر إلى طلوع الشمس.

باب صلاة التطوع

س٥٢: هل تسن صلاة التطوع؟ وما أفضلها ؟

ج: صلاة التطوع مسنونة. وأفضلها ما سن جماعة. وآكدها: الكسوف، فالاستسقاء، فالتراويح، فالوتر. وأقله: ركعة، وأكثره إحدى عشر ركعة، وأدنى الكمال ثلاث ركعات بسلامين. ووقته: ما بين صلاة العشاء وطلوع الفجر، يقنت فيه بعد الركوع، ولو قنت قبله جاز.

Section on the times of ṣalāt

51. What are the timings of ṣalāt?

Ẓuhr is immediately after zenith of the sun until the shadow of an object is the same as the object in addition to the shadow that was present at zenith.

ʿAṣr immediately follows Ẓuhr and the preferred time of ʿAṣr is until the shadow of an object is double the object in addition to the shadow that was present at zenith. Then after this is the time of necessity, and it is ḥarām to delay the time of ʿAṣr until this time. The time of necessity extends until sunset.

Maghrib is after the setting of the sun until the disappearance of the red twilight.

ʿIsha is preferable after the disappearance of the red twilight until the end of the first third of the night. This is followed by the time of necessity which extends until before Fajr.

Ṣubḥ (or Fajr) starts from the start of Fajr (true dawn) until sunrise.

Section on taṭawwuʿ (nafl prayers)

52. Is ṣalāt taṭawwuʿ sunna? Which one is the most virtuous?

Ṣalāt taṭawwuʿ is sunna. The most virtuous are those which are prayed in jamāʿah. The most emphasised is kusūf (eclipse prayer), then istisqā (drought prayer), then tarāwīḥ and then witr. Witr is a minimum of one rakʿat and a maximum of eleven rakʿats. Its time is between ʿIsha and the start of Fajr. Qunūt is done after rukūʿ. However, it is permitted before rukūʿ.

والوارد فيه أن يقول: اللهم اهدنا فيمن هديت، وعافنا فيمن عافيت، وتولنا فيمن توليت، وبارك لنا ما أعطيت، وقنا شر ما قضيت إنك تقضي ولا يقضى عليك، وإنه لا يذل من واليت، ولا يعز من عاديت، تباركت ربنا وتعاليت. اللهم إنا نعوذ برضاك من سخطك، وبعفوك من عقوبتك، وبك منك، لا نحصي ثناء عليك أنت كما أثنيت على نفسك. وصلى الله على محمد النبي الأمي وعلى آله وصحبه.

ويؤمن المأموم.

ويكون رافعا يديه من أول الدعاء.

وفي آخره يمسح بهما وجهه.

س٥٣: كم هي السنن الرواتب المؤكدة؟

ج: السنن الرواتب المؤكدة عشر ركعات: ركعتان قبل الظهر، وركعتان بعدها، وركعتان بعد المغرب، وركعتان بعد العشاء، وركعتان قبل صلاة الصبح. و يسن قضاؤها، وقضاء الوتر إن فاتت.

س٥٤: ما هي صلاة التراويح؟ وما وقتها؟

ج: صلاة التراويح عشرون ركعة، تصلى ركعتين ركعتين في رمضان. ووقتها ما بين صلاة العشاء والوتر. والأفضل تقديم سنة العشاء عليها.

The duʿā for qunūt is[12]:

اَللَّهُمَّ اهْدِنَا فِيمَنْ هَدَيْتَ، وَعَافِنَا فِيمَنْ عَافَيْتَ، وَتَوَلَّنَا فِيمَنْ تَوَلَّيْتَ، وَبَارِكْ لَنَا مَا أَعْطَيْتَ، وَقِنَا شَرَّ مَا قَضَيْتَ إِنَّكَ تَقْضِيْ وَلَا يُقضَى عَلَيْكَ، وَإِنَّهُ لَا يُذَلُّ مَنْ وَالَيْتَ، وَلَا يَعِزُّ مَنْ عَادَيْتَ، تَبَارَكْتَ رَبَّنَا وَتَعَالَيْتَ. اَللَّهُمَّ إِنَّا نَعُوْذُ بِرِضَاكَ مِنْ سَخَطِكَ، وَبِعَفْوِكَ مِنْ عُقُوْبَتِكَ، وَبِكَ مِنْكَ، لَا نُحْصِي ثَنَاءً عَلَيْكَ أَنْتَ كَمَا أَثْنَيْتَ عَلَى نَفْسِكَ. وَصَلَّى اللهُ عَلَى مُحَمَّدٍ النَّبِيِّ الْأُمِّيِّ وَعَلَى آلِهِ وَصَحْبِهِ.

O Allah, guide us among those whom You have guided, protect us among those whom You have protected, befriend us among those whom You have befriended; grant us blessings in what You have given, save us from the evil You have decreed. For indeed, You decree and none decrees against You. Never is he disgraced whom You take as a friend; and never does he gain respect whom You oppose. Blessed and exalted are You our Lord. O Allah, we seek refuge in your pardon from Your punishment, and we seek refuge in You from You, we are not capable of extolling You as You have extolled Yourself. May Allah send ṣalāt upon Muḥammad the Unlettered Prophet and upon his family and companions.

Hands are raised from the beginning of the above duʿā and at the end the face is wiped with them.

53. What are the emphasised rawātib sunnas?

There are ten rawātib muʾakkada sunnas (emphasised sunnas performed with farḍ prayers): two rakʿats before Ẓuhr, two rakʿats after it, two rakʿats after maghrib, two rakʿats after ʿIsha and two rakʿats before Fajr. It is sunna to make qaḍā of these and witr if missed.

54. How many rakʿats is tarawīḥ and when is it performed?

Tarawīḥ prayers consists of twenty rakʿats. They are prayed in twos during Ramaḍān between ʿIsha and witr. It is preferred that the sunna of ʿIsha are prayed before tarawīḥ.

---

[12] Duʿā qunūt has several variations. Here it is in the plural form (double lineed), when praying individually one will say نِيْ instead of نَا. The words نَعُوْذُ and نُحْصِي (with single line) when praying individually are recited أَعُوْذُ and أُحْصِي. The words with a squiggly line beneath it i.e. يُذَلُّ and يَعِزُّ can also be recited as يُذِلُّ and يُعِزُّ.

باب شروط الصلاة

س٥٥: شروط الصلاة كم؟ وما هي؟

ج: شروط الصلاة تسعة، وهي:

١. الإسلام.

٢. والعقل.

٣. والتمييز.

٤. والطهارة مع القدرة عليها.

٥. ودخول الوقت.

٦. وستر العورة مع القدرة بشيء لا يصف البشرة.

٧. واجتناب النجاسة التي لم يعف عنها لبدن المصلي، وثوبه، وبقعته، مع القدرة.

٨. واستقبال القبلة مع الإمكان.

٩. والنية.

باب أركان الصلاة

س٥٦: أركان الصلاة كم؟ وما هي؟

ج: أركان الصلاة أربعة عشر ركنا، وهي:

١. القيام في الفرض على القادر منتصبا.

Section on the prerequisites of ṣalāt

55. How many prerequisites are there for ṣalāt and what are they?

There are nine prerequisites for ṣalāt:

a. Islām

b. being of sound mind

c. discernment

d. being in a state of purity when one is able to do so

e. entering of the ṣalāt time

f. covering of the ʿawra (part of the body that needs to be covered for ṣalāt)

g. avoiding filth which may not be overlooked whether it be on the body of the worshipper or on his clothing or the place of prayer when one is able to do so

h. facing the Qibla when possible

i. intention

Section on the arkān (farḍ acts) of Ṣalāt

56. How many arkān of ṣalāt are there? What are they?

There are fourteen arkān of ṣalāt:

a. qiyām or standing upright for one who is able

٢. وتكبيرة الإحرام.

٣. وقراءة الفاتحة، مرتبة، وفيها إحدى عشرة تشديدة. فإن ترك واحدة منها ، أو ترك حرفا ولم يأت بما ترك لم تصح الصلاة، فإن لم يعرف إلا آية كررها بقدر الفاتحة.

٤. والركوع.

٥. والرفع منه بقصده.

٦. والاعتدال قائما .

٧. والسجود .

٨. والرفع منه.

٩. والجلوس بين السجدتين.

١٠. والطمأنينة - أي السكون - في كل ركن فعلي.

١١. والتشهد الأخير، وهو اللهم صل على محمد بعد الإتيان بالتشهد الأوّل.

١٢. والجلوس للتشهد، وللتسليمتين.

١٣. والتسليمتان في الفرض بأن يقول: السلام عليكم ورحمة الله مرتين، أما في النفل والجنازة فيكفي تسليمة واحدة.

١٤. وترتيب الأركان - كما ذكرت هنا.

b. the opening takbīr i.e. to say Allāhu Akbar

c. reading Fātiḥa in the correct order with the eleven shaddas. If even one shadda is omitted or a letter is left out and he does not go back to correct it, the ṣalāt will be invalid. If one does not know Fātiḥa and knows only one ayat, then he must repeat that for the duration of reciting Fātiḥa

d. rukūʿ or bowing

e. raising from rukūʿ with intent[13]

f. iʿtidāl or pausing while standing

g. sujūd or prostration

h. raising from sujūd.

i. sitting between the two sajdas

j. to conduct all the arkān actions calmly

k. the last tashahhud i.e. اَللّٰهُمَّ صَلِّ عَلَى مُحَمَّد which will follow the first tashahhud (in a three or four rakʿat ṣalāt).

l. sitting for tashahhud and sitting for two salāms

m. two salāms in the farḍ ṣalāt which is to say اَلسَّلَامُ عَلَيْكُمْ وَرَحْمَةُ الله. As for nafl and janāza prayers, saying one salām is sufficient.

n. performing the arkān in order as mentioned above

[13] If one gets up from rukūʿ out of fear or in reaction to something else that he has seen, then this cannot be considered getting up from rukūʿ.

باب واجبات الصلاة

س٥٨: واجبات الصلاة كم؟ وما هي؟

ج: واجبات الصلاة ثمانية، وهي:

١. التكبير لغير الإحرام.
٢. وقول: سمع الله لمن حمده للإمام والمنفرد.
٣. وقول: ربنا ولك الحمد للإمام والمأموم والمنفرد.
٤. وقول: سبحان ربي العظيم مرة في الركوع.
٥. وقول: سبحان ربي الأعلى مرة في السجود.
٦. وقول: رب اغفر لي مرة بين السجدتين.
٧. والتشهد الأول.
٨. والجلوس له.

وهو: التَّحِيَّاتُ لِلهِ وَالصَّلَوَاتُ والطَّيِّبَاتُ، السَّلَامُ عَلَيْكَ أَيُّهَا النَّبِيُّ وَرَحْمَةُ اللهِ وَبَرَكَاتُهُ، السَّلَامُ عَلَيْنَا وَعَلَى عِبَادِ اللَّهِ الصَّالِحِينَ أَشْهَدُ أَنْ لَا إِلَهَ إِلَّا اللهُ، وَأَشْهَدُ أَنَّ مُحَمَّدًا عَبْدُهُ وَرَسُولُهُ.

باب سنن الصلاة

س٥٨: ما سنن الصلاة القولية؟

ج: سنن الصلاة القولية: منها:

Wājibāt of Ṣalāt

57. How many wājibs of ṣalāt are there? What are they?

There are eight wājibs of ṣalāt. They are:

a. takbīr other than the opening takbīr.
b. saying سَمِعَ اللهُ لِمَنْ حَمِدَهُ *Allāh has heard the one who praises him* by the imām and the individual worshipper
c. saying رَبَّنَا وَلَكَ الْحَمْدُ *Our Lord! And for you is all praise* by the imām, the follower and the individual worshipper
d. saying سُبْحَانَ رَبِّيَ الْعَظِيْم *My Lord the Greatest is free from imperfection* once in rukūʿ
e. saying سُبْحَانَ رَبِّيَ الْأَعْلى *My Lord the Loftiest is free from imperfection* once in sujūd
f. saying رَبِّ أغْفِرلِي *My Lord, forgive me* once between the sajdas.
g. the first tashahhud
h. sitting for the first tashahhud

Tashahhud is to say: (Arabic on opposite page) *Salutations are for Allāh. All acts of worship and good deeds are for Him. Peace, mercy and blessings of Allāh be upon you O Prophet. Peace be upon us and upon all of Allāh's righteous slaves. I bear witness that none has the right to be worshipped except Allāh and I bear witness that Muhammad is His slave and Messenger.*

Sunnas of ṣalāt

58. What are the verbal sunnas of ṣalāt?

Some of the verbal sunnas of ṣalāt are:

١. دعاء الافتتاح، وهو سبحانك اللهم وبحمدك، وتبارك اسمك، وتعالى جدك، ولا إله غيرك.
٢. والتعوذ.
٣. والبسملة.
٤. وقول آمين بعد الفاتحة.
٥. وقراءة سورة بعدها.
٦. والجهر بالقراءة للإمام في موضعه. ويكره الجهر للمأموم، ويخير المنفرد.
٧. وقول الإمام والمنفرد بعد التحميد: ملء السماوات، وملء الأرض، وملء ما شئت من شيء بعد.
٨. وما زاد على المرة في تسبيح الركوع والسجود، وقول: رب اغفر لي.
٩. والصلاة على آله صلى الله عليه وسلم في التشهد الأخير.
١٠. والبركة عليهم فيه.
١١. والدعاء بعد التشهد الأخير.

س٥٩: ما سنن الصلاة الفعلية؟

ج: سنن الصلاة الفعلية كثيرة، وتسمى الهيئات، منها:

١. رفع اليدين عند تكبيرة الإحرام.
٢. وعند الركوع.
٣. وعند الرفع منه.

a. the opening duʿā: سُبْحَانَكَ اللّٰهُمَّ وَبِحَمْدِكَ وَتَبَارَكَ اسْمُكَ وَتَعَالَى جَدُّكَ وَلاَ إِلٰهَ غَيْرُكَ *Glory and praise be to You Allāh. Blessed be Your name and exalted be Your majesty, there is none worthy of worship except You*
b. saying taʿawwudh
c. saying basmala
d. saying āmīn after Fātiḥa
e. reading a surah after Fātiḥa
f. imām to recite audibly in the appropriate places. Doing so is makrūh for a follower but an individual-worshipper can choose.
g. imām or an individual worshipper can say after taḥmīd (letter *c* on page 70): مِلْءَ السَّمَاوَاتِ وَمِلْءَ الْأَرْضِ وَمِلْءَ مَا شِئْتَ مِنْ شَيْءٍ بَعْدُ *That which would fill the heavens and the earth, that which is between them and that which will please you besides them*
h. tasbīḥ of rukūʿ, sajda and رَبِّ أغْفِرْلِي to be done more than once
i. ṣalāt on the Prophet's family in the last tashahhud.
j. asking baraka for them as well.
k. duʿā after the last tashahhud

59. What are the sunna actions in ṣalāt?

They are many, they are also called Hay-āt (plural of Hay-ʾā):

a. raising hands with the opening takbīr
b. raising hands when going for rukūʿ
c. raising hands rising up from rukūʿ

٤. ووضع اليد اليمنى على اليسرى تحت سترته حال القراءة .
٥. والنظر إلى موضع السجود.
٦. وتخفيف الصلاة إن كان إماما .
٧. وإطالة الركعة الأولى عن الثانية .
٨. والتفرقة بين القدمين شبرا حال القيام .
٩. وقبض الركبتين باليدين حال الركوع .
١٠. وأن يكون رأسه مساويا لظهره .
١١. ومحافاة العضدين على الجنبين، والبطن عن الفخذين .
١٢. والتفريق بين الركبتين .
١٣. ووضع اليدين حذاء المنكبين في السجود .
١٤. ووضع اليدين على الفخذين، مبسوطتين مضمومتي الأصابع في الجلوس بين السجدتين، وفي التشهد .
١٥. ويقبض الخنصر والبنصر من اليمين، ويحلق إبهامها مع الوسطى، ويشير بالسبابة في التشهد عند ذكر كل جلالة .

إلى غير ذلك مما هو مذكور في المطولات.

d. placing the right hand over the left hand under the navel when reciting

e. look at the place of sajda

f. pray a short ṣalāt if one is Imām

g. make the first rakʿat longer than the second.

h. have a gap of one handspan between the feet while standing.

i. grasping the knees during the rukūʿ

j. head is straight with the back (during rukūʿ)

k. have the arms away from the sides and belly from the thighs.

l. to have a gap between the knees

m. have the hands up to the shoulders during sujud

n. place the hands on the thighs when sitting between the sajdas and in tashahhud with hands stretched out and fingers joined together.

o. to clasp the small finger and the ring finger on the right hand and to make a ring of the thumb and middle finger, and to point with the index finger whenever the name of Allāh is mentioned.

There are more details of these (and other sunnas) in larger texts.

باب سجود السهو

س٦٠: ما حكم سجود السهو؟ وما كيفيته؟

ج: يسن سجود السهو إذا أتى المصلي بقول مشروع في غير محله سهوا . ويباح إذا ترك مسنونا . ويجب:

١. إذا زاد ركوعا أو سجودا أو قياما أو قعودا – ولو قدر جلسة الاستراحة.
٢. أو سلم قبل إتمامها .
٣. أو ترك واجبا سهوا .
٤. أو شك في زيادة وقت فعلها .

وكيفيته: أن يسجد سجدتين: إما بعد فراغ التشهد وقبل السلام. وإما بعد السلام من الصلاة، لكنه يتشهد التشهد الأخير ثم يسلم.

باب مكروهات الصلاة

س٦١: ما يكره في الصلاة للمصلي؟

ج: يكره للمصلي:

١. اقتصاره على الفاتحة فيما تسن فيه السورة بعدها .
٢. وتكرارها .
٣. والتفاته في الصلاة بلا حاجة.
٤. وتغميض عينيه .

Section on sujūd sahw

60. What is the ruling on sujūd sahw? How is it to be performed?

Sujūd Sahw is sunna if one utters something (of ṣalāt) in ṣalāt where they should not, forgetfully.

It is mubāḥ to do sujūd sahw for omitting a sunna.

It is wājib when one:

a. performs an extra rakʿat, a sajdah, a standing or sitting (even for a short time such as the duration of jalsa istirāḥa or resting while sitting before getting up for next rakʿat)
b. salām before completion of prayer
c. omitting a wājib forgetfully
d. doubt on whether one has performed an extra act

Method of sajdah sahw: it is to make two sajdas either after tashahhud and before salām or it is after salām of ṣalāt then another final tashahhud is done and another salām is performed.

Section on makrūhāt or disliked acts of ṣalāt

61. What is makrūh in ṣalāt for a worshipper?

It is makrūh:

a. to only read Fātiḥa if it is sunna to read a surah also

b. repetition of surah Fātiḥa

c. looking around along with moving the head without necessity

d. closing one's eyes

٥. وحمل مشغل له.
٦. وافتراش ذراعيه ساجدا.
٧. والعبث.
٨. والتخصر أي وضع يديه على خاصرته.
٩. والتمطي.
١٠. وفتح فمه.
١١. ووضع شيء فيه.
١٢. واستقبال صورة.
١٣. واستقبال وجه آدمي.
١٤. ومتحدث.
١٥. ونائم.
١٦. ونار.
١٧. وما يلهيه.
١٨. ومس الحصى.
١٩. وتسوية التراب بلا عذر.
٢٠. والتروح بمروحة.
٢١. وفرقعة أصابعه.
٢٢. ومس لحيته.
٢٣. وكف ثوبه.

ومتى كثر ذلك عرفا بطلت الصلاة.

e. to carry that which distracts

f. to have forearms stretched out on the ground in sajda

g. fidgeting

h. placing hands on the hips

i. stretching

j. opening one's mouth

k. placing something in the mouth

l. facing an image

m. praying in the direction while a person faces him

n. praying in the direction of someone speaking

o. praying in the direction of someone asleep

p. praying in the direction of a fire

q. praying in the direction of that which diverts his attention

r. touching pebbles

s. levelling soil without need

t. fanning oneself with a fan

u. cracking fingers

v. touching the beard

w. holding one's clothes

If any of these become excessive (normally understood to be so) then ṣalāt is invalidated.

باب مبطلات الصلاة

س٦٢: ما يبطل الصلاة؟

ج: يبطل الصلاة:

١. كل ما أبطل الطهارة.

٢. وكشف العورة عمدا .

٣. واستدبار القبلة مع القدرة على استقبالها .

٤. واتصال النجاسة التي لا يعفى عنها للمصلي إن لم يزلها في الحال.

٥. والعمل الكثير في العادة، من غير جنسها ، في غير صلاة الخوف.

٦. والاستناد قويا لغير عذر.

٧. ورجوعه للتشهد الأول عالما ذاكرا بعد شروعه في القراءة.

٨. وتعمد زيادة ركن فعلي.

٩. وتعمد تقديم بعض الأركان على بعض.

١٠. وتعمد السلام قبل إتمامها .

١١. وتعمد إحالة المعنى في القراءة.

١٢. ووجود سترة بعيدة وهو عريان.

١٣. وفسخ النية.

١٤. والتردد فيه.

Invalidators of Ṣalāt

62. What are the invalidators of ṣalāt?

Salat is invalidated by:

a. everything that invalidates tahāra or purification
b. exposing ʿawra intentionally
c. turning one's back to the Qibla when one is able to face it
d. coming in contact with najāsa that is inexcusable for one doing ṣalāt, if it is not removed immediately
e. customarily excessive movements not part of ṣalāt, other than ṣalāt of khawf
f. leaning by someone who is fit without necessity
g. going back to the first tashahhud by a knowledgeable person who is fully aware after starting qirāʾa (of Fātiḥa in the next rakʿat)
h. intentionally doing an extra rukn action
i. intentionally doing some rukn actions before others
j. intentionally doing salām before completion of ṣalāt.
k. intentionally reciting in a manner that changes the meaning
l. sutra placed far, while one is naked
m. annulling one's intention
n. intending to break one's intention

١٥. والعزم عليه.
١٦. وعملهُ مع الشك في النية.
١٧. والدعاء بملاذ الدنيا.
١٨. والإتيان بكاف الخطاب لغير الله ورسوله.
١٩. والقهقهة.
٢٠. والكلام ولو سهوا.
٢١. وتقدم المأموم على إمامه.
٢٢. وبطلان صلاة إمامه.
٢٣. وسلامه عمدا قبل إمامه، أو سهوا ولم يعده بعده.
٢٤. والأكل.
٢٥. والشرب سوى اليسر عرفا لناس أو جاهل.

ولا تبطل:

١. إن بلع ما بين أسنانه بلا مضغ.
٢. ولا تبطل إن نام نوما يسيرا فتكلم، أو سبق الكلام على لسانه حال قراءته.
٣. أو غلبه سعال أو عطاس، أو تثاؤب، أو بكاء، فبان حرفان.

o. acting with doubt in an intention.

p. wavering in intention

q. du'ā for desires of the world.

r. using the kāf of second person (in Arabic) to other than Allāh ta'āla or His Messenger ﷺ

s. laughing loudly

t. speaking, even if forgetfully

u. follower going in front of the imām

v. imām invalidating his ṣalāt

w. performing salām before the imām intentionally or forgetfully and does not repeat it afterwards (i.e. after the imām's salām)

x. eating

y. drinking except what is customarily understood to be a small
amount or (a large amount) out of ignorance.

However, ṣalāt does not break if one:

a. swallows without chewing what was stuck in one's teeth
b. falls asleep for a small duration and speaks therein or during qirā'a utters something else
c. is overcome by sneezing, yawning or crying and utters two letters

باب صلاة الجماعة

س٦٣: على من تجب صلاة الجماعة؟

ج: تجب صلاة الجماعة للصلوات الخمس على: الرجال الأحرار القادرين عليها، حضرا وسفرا.

ولا تنعقد بالمميز في الفرض.

وتسن الجماعة في المسجد.

وتسن للنساء منفردات عن الرجال.

س٦٤: ما يتحمل الإمام عن المأموم؟

ج: يتحمل الإمام عن المأموم ثمانية أشياء:

١. القراءة.

٢. وسجود السهو.

٣. وسجود التلاوة.

٤. والسترة قدامه، لأن سترة الإمام سترة لمن خلفه.

٥. ودعاء القنوت.

٦. والتشهد الأول إذا سبق المأموم بركعة في رباعية.

٧. وقول: سمع الله لمن حمده.

Section on the jamāʿa or congregational ṣalāt

63. Upon whom is ṣalāt with jamāʿa (congregation) wājib?

Ṣalāt with jamāʿa is wājib for the five times prayers for: free men capable of doing jamāʿa whether they be resident or travelling.

It is not considered a farḍ ṣalāt from a child that has not reached the age of discernment.[14]

It is sunna to pray jamāʿa in a masjid.

It is sunna for women to pray jamāʿa when separate from men.

64. What are the actions of the imām done on behalf of the followers?

The imām is responsible on behalf of the followers for eight things:

a. qirāʾa or recitation
b. sujūd of forgetfulness
c. sujūd of tilāwat
d. sutra to be in front of him, because the sutra of the Imām is a sutra for those praying behind him
e. duʿā of qunūt
f. first tashahhud, if the follower joined after the first rakʿat in a four rakʿat ṣalāt[15]
g. to say سَمِعَ اللّٰهُ لِمَنْ حَمِدَهُ *Allāh has heard the one who praises Him*

---

[14] If two people are praying and a follower is a child, then this is not a jamāʿa.

[15] If a follower misses a rakʿat then in his second rakʿat, he should make tashahhud, but as he is a follower, the imam is taking that responsibility.

٨.   وقول: ملء السماء، وملء الأرض، وملء ما شئت من شيء بعد .

س٦٥: من الأولى بالإمامة؟

ج: الأولى بها:

١. الأجود قراءة. ويقدم قارئ لا يعلم فقه صلاته على فقيه أمي.
٢. ثم الأسن.
٣. ثم الأشرف.
٤. ثم الأتقى والأورع.
٥. ثم يقرع.

وصاحب البيت، وإمام المسجد - ولو عبدا - أحق بالإمامة.
والحر أولى من العبد .
والحاضر والبصير والمتوضئ أولى من ضدهم.
وتكره إمامة غير الأولى بلا إذنه.
ولا تصح إمامة الفاسق مطلقا إلا في جمعة وعيد تعذرا خلف غيره.
ولا تصح إمامة العاجز عن شرط أو ركن إلا بمثله.

h. saying مِلْءَ السَّمَاوَاتِ وَمِلْءَ الْأَرْضِ وَمِلْءَ مَا شِئْتَ مِنْ شَيْءٍ بَعْدُ

65. What is the order of preference for selection of the imām?

The order of preference for selection of the imām should be:

a. the one with the best qirāʾa. The reciter who does not know the fiqh of ṣalāt will be given preference over the one knowledgeable of ṣalāt but cannot recite well.

b. the most senior in age

c. the most noble

d. the most pious and most god-fearing

e. then lots will be drawn.

The man of the house and the appointed imām have the most right to be imām even if they are slaves.

The free man is preferred as imām than a slave.

The resident, the one of sight and one who has wuḍū are preferred than their opposites.

It is makrūh for the non-preferred to lead without permission (of the preferred).

Ṣalāt of a fāsiq (sinner) is absolutely not valid, except in Jumuʿa and ʿĪd where one is excused as he cannot follow someone else, alternatively.

It is not valid for one who is incapable of performing a prerequisite or a rukn to lead someone except if the follower is in the same condition.

ولا تصح إمامة المرأة للرجال، ولا إمامة المميز للبالغ في الفرض، وتصح إمامته في النفل، وفي الفرض بصبي مثله.
ولا يصح الفرض خلف النفل، ويصح العكس.
وتصح المقضية خلف الحاضرة. وعكسه حيث استويا في الاسم، فلا يصح عصر خلف ظهر ولا عكسه.

س٦٦: أين موقف الإمام من المأموم؟

ج: يصح وقوف الإمام وسط المأمومين، والسنة وقوفه مقدما عليهم.
ويقف الرجل الواحد عن يمينه محاذيا له، ولا تصح عن يساره مع خلو يمينه.
وتقف المرأة خلفه.
ولا يصح أن يقف الرجل منفردا خلف الصف.

س٦٧: من يعذر بترك الجمعة والجماعة؟

ج: يعذر بترك الجمعة والجماعة:
١. المريض.
٢. والخائف حدوث المرض.
٣. والمدافع أحد الأخبثين البول والغائط.

It is not valid for a woman to lead men or one who is at the age of discernment to lead (farḍ) the one who has reached the age of puberty. However, he can lead nafl or farḍ for other children.

It is not valid to pray farḍ behind someone praying nafl, but the reverse is valid.

It is permitted to pray qadā ṣalāt behind a current jamāʿa ṣalāt or vice versa as long as they are the same prayer (for example both are praying ʿAṣr, one qadā and one current). However, it is not valid to pray ʿAṣr behind Ẓuhr or vice versa.

66. Where does the imām stand in relation to the follower?

The correct position is to stand in the middle of the row and the sunna is to be in front of the row.

A single follower will stand in line with the imām on his right. It will not be correct to do so on the left while there is no one on the right.

A woman should stand behind a man (leading).

It will not be correct for a single male follower to make his own row behind a row.

67. Who is excused from jumuʿa and jamāʿa?

The following people are excused from attending jumuʿa and jamāʿa:

a. sick person
b. the one who is fearful that he may become sick
c. one who requires to urinate or defecate

٤. ومن له ضائع يرجوه.

٥. أو يخاف ضياع ماله، أو فواته، أو يخاف ضررا فيه.

٦. أو يخاف على مال استؤجر لحفظه كنظارة بستان.

٧. أو أذى بمطر ووحل، أو ثلج وجليد، وريح باردة بليلة مظلمة.

باب الجمع بين الصلاتين

س ٦٨: هل يجوز الجمع بين الصلاتين أم لا؟

ج: يباح الجمع لمسافر والقصر بين الظهر والعصر، وبين العشاءين بوقت أحدهما. ويباح لمقيم مريض يلحقه بتركه مشقة. ولمرضع لمشقة كثرة النجاسة. ولعاجز عن الطهارة لكل صلاة. ويختص بجواز جمع العشاءين - ولو صلى ببيته - ثلج، وجليد، و وحل، وريح شديدة باردة، ومطر يبل الثياب وتوجد معه مشقة. والأفضل: فعل الأوفق من تقديم الجمع وتأخيره.

باب صلاة الجمعة

س٦٩: على من تجب صلاة الجمعة؟

ج: تجب صلاة الجمعة على كل ذكر مكلف، ولا عذر له، وعلى مسافر لا يباح

d. one who is hopeful in attaining something lost
e. one who fears the waste or loss of his wealth or fears harm in that
f. or fears the loss of wealth that he has been hired to guard, such as a guard for an orchard
g. one is harmed by rain or mud, snow or sleet, or a cold wind on a dark night

Joining two ṣalāts

68. Is it allowed to join two prayers?

It is permitted for a traveller to join and shorten the Ẓuhr and ʿAsr prayers and to join and shorten the ʿIsha with the maghrib prayers, in the time of either ṣalāt.

Joining ṣalāts is permitted for a resident sick person if he will experience hardship, one suckling a baby due to excessive najāsa or one incapable of ṭaharah for every ṣalāt.

Joining of Maghrib and ʿIsha is permitted even if he prays in his own home, with the condition there is snow, sleet, strong and cold wind, rain that will wet the clothes. It is wājib that there must exist hardship in all of these. The best thing is to join the prayers when it is most convenient, whether it be during the first ṣalāt's time or the second.

Jumuʿa Salat

69. Upon whom is Jumuʿa wājib?

Jumuʿa is wājib upon every legally obligated male, without an excuse, and upon a traveller who is not travelling the distance that allows him

له القصر وتجب على مقيم خارج البلد إذا كان بينه وبين محل قيامها وفعلها فرسخ، فأقل من فرسخ. وهي ركعتان.

س٧٠: ما شروط صحة صلاة الجمعة؟

ج: شروط صحة صلاة الجمعة أربعة، وهي:

١. الوقت: أي من وقت صلاة الضحى إلى آخر وقت الظهر.
٢. وأن تكون بقرية يستوطنها أربعون رجلا.
٣. وحضور أربعين رجلا ممن تجب عليهم - ولو بالإمام.
٤. وتقدم خطبتين.

س٧١: ما شروط الخطبتين؟

ج: شروط الخطبتين خمسة، وهي:

١. الوقت.
٢. والنية.
٣. ووقوعها حضرا.
٤. وحضور أربعين رجلا ممن تجب عليهم.
٥. وأن يكون الخطيب ممن تصح إمامته فيها.

to shorten prayers, upon a resident who leaves his land and between him and his place of resident and the Jumuʿa is a distance of one farsakh (one parasang or approximately 5.5 kms) or less than that. Jumuʿa ṣalāt is two rakʿat.

70. What are the requisites for the soundness of ṣalāt Jumuʿa?

The soundness of the ṣalāt Jumuʿa is four:

a. time: from the time of Ḍuḥa until the end of Ẓuhr
b. a village inhabited by forty Muslim men
c. presence of forty men upon whom Jumuʿa is wājib including the imām
d. to precede the ṣalāt with two khutbas

71. What the requisites for the two khutbas?

There are five requisites for the two khutbas:

a. time
b. intention
c. to be done by those who are resident (not a group of travellers)
d. presence of forty men upon whom it is wājib
e. the khatīb be one whose leading of jumuʿa ṣalāt is valid

س٧٢: ما أركان الخطبتين؟

ج: أركان الخطبتين ستة، وهي:

١. حمد الله تعالى.

٢. والصلاة على رسوله صلى الله عليه وسلم.

٣. وقراءة آية من كتاب الله تعالى.

٤. والوصية بتقوى الله – جل شأنه.

٥. وموالاتهما مع الصلاة.

٦. والجهر بهما بحيث يسمع العدد المعتبر، حيث لا مانع.

ويحرم على سامعهما الكلام، ولو قرآنا.

س٧٣: ما سنن الخطبتين؟

ج: سننهما:

١. الطهارة.

٢. وستر العورة.

٣. وإزالة النجاسة.

٤. والدعاء للمسلمين.

٥. وأن يتولاهما واحد.

72. What are the arkān of the khutbas?

The arkān of the two khutbas are:

a. praise Allāh taʿāla

b. ṣalāt on the Prophet ﷺ

c. reciting a verse from the Book of Allāh

d. to enjoin taqwa of Allāh ﷻ

e. to be done immediately before the ṣalāt

f. to be audible so a substantial number of people can hear it as long as there is nothing to prevent that.

It is ḥarām upon those who hear it to speak even if it is a verse.

73. What are the sunnas of the two khutbas?

Its sunnas are to:

a. perform tahāra
b. cover the ʿawra
c. remove of najāsa
d. make duʿā for the Muslims
e. be done by one person

٦. ورفع الصوت بهما حسب الطاقة.
٧. وأن يخطب قائما على مرتفع، معتمدا على سيف أو عصا.
٨. وأن يجلس بينهما، فإن أبى أن يجلس، أو خطب جالسا سكت قليلا.
٩. وقصرهما.
١٠. وكون الثانية أقصر.

س٧٤: هل يجوز تعدد الجمعة والعيد في البلد؟

ج: تحرم إقامة الجمعة والعيد في أكثر من موضع من البلد إلا لحاجة كضيق المسجد وكبعده عن بعض أهل البلد وكخوف فتنة.

فإن تعددت لغير عذر فالسابقة بالإحرام هي الصحيحة.

باب صلاة العيدين

س٧٥: ما حكم صلاة العيدين؟ وما شروطها؟ وما وقتها؟

ج: صلاة العيدين فرض كفاية. وشروطها كشروط الجمعة، من التوطن والعدد، ما عدا الخطبتين، فإنهما سنة.

ووقتها: من ارتفاع الشمس قدر رمح إلى قبيل الزوال.

وهي بلا أذان ولا إقامة، بل ينادى لها: الصلاة جامعة ثلاثا.

f. raise one's voice as much as possible
g. deliver khutbah standing from an elevated place and to be leaning on a sword or staff.
h. sit between the two khutbas. If one does not sit or is doing the khutbas seated then he should remain silent for a little while between the khutbas.
i. make both khutbas short.
j. make the second khutbah shorter.

74. Are multiple jumuʿa and ʿĪd ṣalāts permitted in one area?

It is ḥarām to establish multiple jumuʿa and ʿĪd ṣalāts in a single locality without necessity such as a masjid being too small, it is too far or fear of fitna.
If they become numerous without need then the first one is the correct one to pray in.

Ṣalāt of the two ʿĪds

75. What is the ruling of the two ʿĪd ṣalāts? What are their prerequisites? What are their timings?

Both ʿĪd ṣalāts are farḍ kifāya. Its prerequisites are the same as jumuʿa in terms of the type of area and number people required, except for the two khutbas, which are sunna.

Their timings are from the rising of the sun when it is a spears length high and extends until just before midday.

It has no athān or iqāma but the announcement "Aṣ-ṣalātu jāmiʿah" can be made three times.

س٧٦: كيف صفة صلاة العيد ؟

ج: صلاة العيد ركعتان، يكبر في الأولى بعد تكبيرة الإحرام ودعاء الافتتاح، وقبل التعوذ، ست تكبيرات، وفي الثانية بعد القيام من السجود وقبل القراءة خمسا، يرفع يديه مع كل تكبيرة ويقول بين كل تكبيرتين: الله أكبر كبيرا، والحمد لله كثيرا، وسبحان الله بكرة وأصيلا، وصلى الله على سيدنا محمد النبي الأمي وعلى آله وصحبه وسلم تسليما كثيرا.

ثم يستعيذ في الأولى، ويقرأ الفاتحة جهرا، ثم سورة ﴿سبح اسم ربك الأعلى﴾ وفي الثانية سورة الغاشية.

فإذا سلم الإمام خطب خطبتين كخطبتي الجمعة في جميع الأحكام، لكن يبتدئ الخطبة الأولى بتسع تكبيرات، والثانية بسبع.

وإن صلى العيد كالنافلة صح.

س٧٧: ما التكبير المطلق والمقيد وما حكمهما ؟

ج: يسن التكبير المطلق والجهر به في ليلة العيدين إلى فراغ الخطبة، وفي كل عشر ذي الحجة.

والتكبير المقيد من فجر يوم عرفة إلى عصر آخر أيام التشريق بعد كل صلاة صليت بالجماعة.

وصفته: الله أكبر، الله أكبر، لا إله إلا الله، والله أكبر، الله أكبر، ولله الحمد.

76. What is the description of the Ṣalāt of ʿĪd?

Ṣalāt of ʿĪd consists of two rakʿats. In the first rakʿat after the opening takbīr and opening duʿā i.e. before taʿawwudh there are six takbīrs. In the second rakʿat when one gets up from sujūd and before beginning reciting, there are five takbīrs. The hands are raised with every takbīr and in between takbīrs the following is said: اللّٰهُ أَكْبَرُ كَبِيرًا وَالْحَمْدُ لِلّٰهِ كَثِيرًا وَسُبْحَانَ اللّٰهِ بُكْرَةً وَأَصِيلًا اللّٰهُ وَصَلَّى اللهُ عَلَى سَيِّدِنَا مُحَمَّدٍ النَّبِيِّ الْأُمِّيِّ وَعَلَى آلِهِ وَصَحْبِهِ وَسَلَّمْ تَسْلِيْمًا كَثِيْرًا *Allāh is most Great, much praise be to Allāh and glory be to Allāh at the beginning and end of the day and confer blessings upon our master Muḥammad, the unlettered Prophet, his followers and companions and confer abundant salutations.*

One says taʿawwudh, then audibly recites Fātiḥa and surah Al-Aʿlā in the first rakʿat. In the second rakʿat surah Ghāshiya is recited.

After the imām says salām, he delivers both khutbahs like the khutbahs of jumuʿa with the same ruling of jumuʿa khutbah. However, he starts the first khutbah with nine takbīrs and the second khutbah with seven takbīrs. However, if ʿĪd ṣalāt is prayed like a nafl prayer (i.e. no additional takbīrs) then it will be valid.

77. What are restricted and unrestricted takbīrs?

It is sunna to do general takbīrs audibly on the nights preceding ʿĪds until the end of the khutbas and in all the ten days of Dhul Ḥijjah.

Specific takbīrs are from the Fajr of the day of ʿArafa until the last ʿAṣr of the days of tashrīq (11-13 of Dhul Ḥijjah) after every ṣalāt prayed in jamāʿa.

Its form is: اللّٰهُ أَكْبَرُ، أللّٰهُ أَكْبَرُ، لَا إِلَهَ إِلَّا اللّٰهُ، وَاللّٰهُ أَكْبَرُ، آللّٰهُ أَكْبَرُ، وَلِلّٰهِ الْحَمْد *Allāh is the greatest, Allāh is the greatest, there is none worthy of worship except for Allāh, and Allāh is the greatest, Allāh is the greatest and to Him belongs all praises.*

س٧٨: كيف حكم الأضحية؟

ج: الأضحية سنة مؤكدة. ويجزئ في الأضحية: من المعز ما له سنة، ومن الضأن ما له نصف سنة، ومن البقر والجاموس ما له سنتان، ومن الإبل ما له خمس سنين. ووقتها من بعد أسبق صلاة العيد إلى آخر ثاني أيام التشريق.

باب أوقات النهي

س٧٩: ما هي الأوقات التي تحرم الصلاة فيها ولا تصح؟

ج: الأوقات المنهي عن صلاة النفل فيها ثلاثة، هي:

١. من طلوع الفجر الثاني إلى ارتفاع الشمس قدر رمح في رأي العين.

٢. ومن صلاة العصر - ولو مجموعة مع الظهر في وقت الظهر إلى غروب الشمس.

٣. وعند قيام الشمس في وسط السماء إلى أن تزول.

سوى: سنة الفجر، وركعتي الطواف، وسنة الظهر بعد العصر لمن جمع.

وسوى: إعادة جماعة أقيمت وهو في المسجد.

78. What is the ruling of uḍḥiya?

Uḍḥiya (qurbāni or sacrifice) is sunna mu'akkada.

Acceptable uḍḥiya is a year-old goat, or six-month-old lamb, or a two-year-old cow or buffalo or a five-year-old camel.

Its timing is after the ʿĪd ṣalāt until the second day of tashrīq (i.e. 12th).

Prohibited times of prayer

79. In which times is ṣalāt prohibited and not prohibited?

The prohibited times of nafl are three:

a. from the start of the second Fajr i.e. true dawn until the sun has risen a spear length according to eyesight.
b. after Ṣalāt ʿAṣr even if joined with Ẓuhr in the time of Ẓuhr until sunset.
c. when the sun is at its zenith until it declines.

An exception to this is the sunnas of Fajr, two rakʿats of tawāf and the sunnas of Ẓuhr after the ʿAṣr for someone who joins (Ẓuhr and ʿAṣr prayers).

Another exception is if following a jamāʿa which has started in the masjid and one has already prayed that ṣalāt.

كتاب الجنائز

باب أحكام الميت

س٨٠: كيف أحكام الميت؟

ج: يجب للميت خمسة أشياء، وهي:

١. غسله.

٢. وتكفينه.

٣. والصلاة عليه.

٤. وحمله.

٥. ودفنه.

ويسن تكفين الرجل في ثلاث لفائف بيض من قطن. والأنثى في خمسة أثواب كذلك. والصبي في ثوب. والصغيرة في ثلاث.

باب أحكام الصلاة على الميت

س٨١: كم شروط الصلاة على الميت؟

ج: شروط الصلاة على الميت ثمانية، وهي:

١. النية.

٢. والتكليف.

Chapter on Janāzas (Funerals)

Section on the rulings for the deceased

80. What are the rulings of the deceased?

There are five things that are wājib to be done for the dead:

a. bathing him (ghusl)
b. shrouding (kafn)
c. ṣalāt (of janāza) for him
d. carrying the body
e. burial

It is sunna to shroud a man in three white cotton wraps and a woman in five. A child is wrapped in one sheet. And a small girl in three.

Ṣalāt of janāza

81. How many prerequisites are there for ṣalāt upon the deceased?

There are eight prerequisites for the ṣalāt upon the deceased:

a. intention

b. to be legally obligated

٣. واستقبال القبلة.

٤. وسترة العورة.

٥. واجتناب النجاسة.

٦. وحضور الميت بين يدي المصلي.

٧. وإسلام المصلى عليه.

٨. وطهارتهما.

س٨٢: كم هي أركان الصلاة على الميت؟

ج: أركان الصلاة على الميت سبعة، وهي:

١. القيام في فرضها. أعني به أول صلاة تصلى عليه.

٢. والتكبيرات الأربع.

٣. وقراءة الفاتحة.

٤. والصلاة على النبي صلى الله عليه وسلم.

٥. والدعاء للميت. وأقله: اللهم اغفر له وارحمه.

٦. والسلام.

٧. والترتيب للأركان.

c. facing the Qibla
d. cover the ʿawra
e. avoid najāsa
f. the deceased to be in front of the worshipper
g. the deceased to be a Muslim
h. both the deceased and the worshipper to be ṭāhir.

82. How many arkān does ṣalāt of janāza have?

There are seven arkān of ṣalāt of janāza:

a. to stand for the farḍ (of janāza). This is for the first ṣalāt of janāza (if there are multiple ones).
b. four takbīrs
c. reading Fātiḥa
d. ṣalāt on the prophet ﷺ
e. to pray for the deceased. The minimum of which can be: اَللَّهُمَّ اغْفِرْ لَهُ وَارحَمْهُ O Allah! Forgive him and have mercy upon him.
f. to do salām
g. to do the arkān in order

س٨٣: كيف صفة الصلاة على الميت؟

ج: صفة الصلاة على الميت:

١. أن يقف عند وسط أنثى، وصدر ذكر.
٢. ويكبر التكبيرة الأولى.
٣. ثم يتعوذ.
٤. ويبسمل.
٥. ويقرأ الفاتحة.
٦. ثم يكبر الثانية، ويصلي على النبي صلى الله عليه وسلم بالصلاة الإبراهيمية.
٧. ثم يكبر الثالثة، ويدعو للميت.
٨. ثم يكبر الرابعة، ويقف قليلا ويسلم.

83. What is the complete description of the janāza ṣalāt?

The description of the janāza ṣalāt is:

a. for the imām to stand at the middle of a female and at the chest of a male
b. make the first takbīr
c. say taʿawwudh
d. say Bismillāh
e. recite Fātiḥa
f. say the second takbīr and then read Ṣalāt Ibrāhīmiyya on the Prophet ﷺ
g. do a third takbīr and then make duʿā for the deceased
h. do a fourth takbīr and then pause briefly and then do salām

كتاب الصيام

باب أحكام الصوم

س٨٤: بم يجب صوم رمضان؟

ج: يجب صوم رمضان برؤية هلاله.

وتثبت رؤيته بخبر مسلم مكلف عدل - احتياطا للعبادة - ولو عبدا أو أنثى.

ولا يكفي في ثبوت غيره من الشهور إلا رجلان عدلان.

س٨٥: ما هي شروط وجوب صوم رمضان؟

ج: شروط وجوب صوم رمضان أربعة أشياء وهي:

١. الإسلام.

٢. والبلوغ.

٣. والعقل.

٤. والقدرة عليه.

س٨٦: ما هي شروط صحة صوم رمضان؟

ج: شروط صحة صوم رمضان ستة أشياء، وهي:

١. الإسلام.

٢. وانقطاع دم الحيض.

Chapter on Fasting

Section on the rulings of fasting

84. What makes fasting of Ramaḍān wājib?

The sighting of the hilāl (new crescent moon) makes fasting wājib.

Hilāl sighting (for the beginning of Ramaḍān) is established by the testimony of one upright and legally obligated person who sees the moon. This is to be cautious in worship (so not to miss a fast of Ramaḍān). The witness can be a slave or female.

However, this will not suffice for other months except with two upright males.

85. Which prerequisites of the fast of Ramaḍān make it wājib?

Four things make the fast of Ramaḍān wājib:

a. Islām

b. passed the age of puberty

c. being of sound mind

d. being capable of fasting

86. What are the prerequisites for a sound of the Ramaḍān fast?

The prerequisites for the soundness the Ramaḍān fast are six:

a. Islām

b. ceasing of menses

٣. والنفاس.
٤. والتمييز.
٥. والعقل.
٦. والنية ليلا لصوم كل يوم واجب.

وفرضه: الإمساك عن جميع المفطرات من طلوع الفجر الثاني إلى إتمام غروب الشمس.

س٨٧: هل يجوز الفطر في رمضان لأحد؟

ج: يجوز الفطر في رمضان لحامل ومرضع خافتا على نفسيهما، ويجب عليهما القضاء فقط. أو خافتا على الولد لزمهما القضاء، ولزم ولي الولد إطعام مسكين لكل يوم مد قمح.

ويجوز الفطر لشيخ كبير.

ويسن لمريض ومسافر سفر القصر.

ويلزم الشيخ الكبير إطعام مسكين لكل يوم.

ويقضي المريض والمسافر بدون إطعام.

باب مفسدات الصوم

س٨٨: ما يفسد الصوم؟

ج: يفسد الصوم اثنا عشر شيئًا، وهي:

c. nifās

d. age of discernment

e. being of sound mind

f. to make intention the night before the fast starts (up to ṣubḥ ṣādiq) for each day is wājib.

Its farḍ is to refrain from all nullifiers of the fast from the start of Fajr until the completion of sunset.

87. Is it allowed for anyone to not fast in Ramadan?

It is permissible for a pregnant or breastfeeding woman, if they both fear for their own lives to not fast. They merely have to make qaḍā later on. If they both fear for the child, then they can also break the fast and make qaḍā later on. Also, in this case the guardian of the child (usually the father) must feed a poor person a *mudd* (approx. half a kilogram) of wheat every day.

It is permitted for an elderly person to not fast.

It is sunna for a sick person or traveller to not fast.

An elderly person (incapable of fasting) must feed a poor person for each day missed.

The sick person and traveller can make up the fast without feeding the poor.

The nullifiers of fasts

88. What nullifies the fast?

Twelve things nullify a fast. They are:

١. خروج دم الحيض.
٢. والنفاس.
٣. والموت.
٤. والردة عن الإسلام والعياذ بالله تعالى.
٥. والعزم على الفطر.
٦. والتردد فيه.
٧. والقيء عمدا.
٨. والاحتقان من الدبر.
٩. وبلع النخامة إذا وصلت إلى الفم.
١٠. وإخراج الدم بالحجامة خاصة - في حق الحاجم والمحجوم.
١١. وإنزال المني، بتكرار النظر، لا بتفكر، ولا باحتلام. وخروج المني أو المذي بتقبيل، أو لمس، أو استمناء، أو مباشرة غير الفرج.
١٢. وكل ما وصل إلى الجوف، والحلق، والدماغ، من مائع أو غيره، مغذيا كان أو لا.

عامدا في الكل لا ناسيا، ولا مكرها، إلا في الجماع فإنه لا يتأتى الإكراه فيه بالنسبة للمجامع.

a. menses

b. nifās

c. death

d. becoming murtad (apostate), with Allāh Taʿāla is refuge!

e. determined to break it

f. wavering in breaking it

g. vomiting intentionally

h. inserting something into the anus

i. swallowing phlegm after it is out in the mouth

j. bleeding by cupping specifically, for both the cupper and cupped

k. ejaculating from repeated looking but not by thinking or a wet dream. Also (the fast is broken) from the exiting of semen, or madhī (pre-coital fluid) due to kissing, touching, masturbation or lovemaking without intercourse

l. anything that reaches the internal cavity (of the torso food or air pipe via mouth), the brain (inside the ears, eyes and nose) whether it be liquid or anything else, nourishing or otherwise

All the above twelve must be intentional not forgetful or forced (except for intercourse by the male, because that can't be by force).

س٨٩: ما الذي يجب بالفطر في رمضان عمدا ؟

ج: يجب بالفطر في رمضان عمدا القضاء .

ولا كفارة إلا بالجماع فيه، على الواطئ والموطوء باختياره.

والكفارة هي:

١ . عتق رقبة مؤمنة .

٢ . فإن لم يستطع فصيام شهرين متتابعين .

٣ . فإن لم يستطع فإطعام ستين مسكينا .

٤ . فإن لم يستطع سقطت .

89. What is wājib if one breaks his fast during Ramaḍān intentionally?

Qaḍā is wājib for the one who breaks his fast in Ramaḍān intentionally.

There is no kafāra (expiation) except for intercourse and that too for the perpetrator of intercourse not the one forced to participate unless they also choose to do so.

Kafāra is:

a. to free a believing slave
b. if not able to do it then fast for two months
c. if not able to do that then feed sixty poor people
d. if that is not possible then doing kafāra is excused

كتاب الزكاة

باب أحكام الزكاة

س٩٠: في أي شيء تجب الزكاة؟

ج: تجب الزكاة في خمسة أشياء:

الأول: بهيمة الأنعام – وهي الإبل والبقر والغنم.

والثاني: الخارج من الأرض.

والثالث: العسل.

والرابع: الذهب والفضة.

والخامس: عروض التجارة – أي البضاعة المعدة للبيع والشراء لأجل الربح.

س٩١: كم هي شروط وجوب الزكاة؟

ج: شروط وجوب الزكاة خمسة أشياء:

الأول: الإسلام.

الثاني: الحرية.

والثالث: ملك النصاب.

والرابع: الملك التام، فلا زكاة على السيد في مال الكتابة، ولا في حصة المضارب قبل القسمة.

والخامس: تمام الحول.

تجب في مال الصغير والمجنون.

Chapter on Zakāt
Section on the rulings of Zakāt

90. For what things is Zakāt wājib?

Zakāt is wājib for five things:

a. livestock: camels, cows, goats and sheep

b. that which is harvested from the ground

c. honey

d. gold and silver

e. merchandise i.e. goods purchased for sale at a profit.

91. What are the prerequisites that make Zakāt wājib?

The prerequisites that make Zakāt wājib are:

a. Islām

b. to be free

c. possess niṣāb

d. complete possession: there is no Zakāt on a slave owner in contract with a slave where he buys his freedom nor upon a business partner before the profits are distributed to each partner

e. completion of a year

Zakāt is also wājib on the wealth of a child and an insane person.

باب زكاة بهيمة الأنعام

س٩٢: كم هي شروط الزكاة في بهيمة الأنعام؟

ج: شروط وجوب الزكاة في بهيمة الأنعام ثلاثة: الأول: أن تتخذ للتربية واللبن والولد، لا للعمل. والثاني: أن ترعى المباح أكثر السنة. والثالث: أن تبلغ نصابا.

س٩٣: كم هو نصاب الإبل؟

ج: أقل نصاب الإبل: خمس، وفيها شاة. ثم في كل خمس شاة. إلى خمس وعشرين وفيها: بنت مخاض، وهي ما تم لها سنة. وفي ست وثلاثين بنت لبون، وهي ما تم لها سنتان. وفي ست وأربعين حقة، لها ثلاث سنين. وفي إحدى وستين جذعة، لها أربع سنين. وفي ست وسبعين بنتا لبون. إلى مائة وثلاثين فيستقر في كل أربعين بنت لبون، وفي كل خمسين حقة.

س٩٤: كم هو نصاب البقر؟

ج: أقل نصاب البقر ثلاثون، وفيها تبيع ذو سنة. وفي أربعين مسنة لها سنتان.

Zakāt of livestock

92. What are the prerequisites of Zakāt for livestock?

The prerequisites of Zakāt for livestock are three:

a. the livestock is for breeding (male), dairy or giving birth to offspring (rearing female livestock)
b. to graze most of the year what grows naturally (without human effort e.g. grass in a field that grows due to rain).
c. to reach the niṣāb amount

93. How much is the niṣāb for camels?

The minimum niṣāb for camels is five camels, and its Zakāt is one sheep. Then for every additional five, it is one sheep until twenty-five. For twenty-five camels and onwards, it is one bint mukhād (a year-old camel). From thirty-six camels and onwards, it is a bint labūn (two-year-old camel). From forty-six camels and onwards, it is a ḥiqqa (a three-year-old camel). From sixty-one camels and onwards, it is a jizʿa (four-year-old camel).

From seventy-six camels and onwards, it is two bint labūns or two two-year-old camels.

From a hundred and thirty onwards, for every forty is a bint labūn (two-year-old camel) and for every fifty is a ḥiqqa (three-year-old camel).

94. What is the niṣāb for cows?

The minimum niṣāb for a cow is thirty for which Zakāt is one tabīʿ (one-year old calf). For forty cows it is a musinna (two-year-old cow).

س٩٥: كم هو نصاب الغنم؟ وما حكم الخليطين؟

ج: أقل نصاب الغنم أربعون، وفيها شاة معز تم لها سنة، أو جذعة ضأن لها ستة أشهر. و في مائة وإحدى وعشرين شاتان، وفي مائتين وواحدة ثلاث شياه، وفي أربعمائة أربع شياه.

ثم في كل مائة شاة شاة واحدة.

وإذا اختلط اثنان فأكثر في نصاب ماشية جميع الحول، واشتركا في المبيت والمسرح والمحلب والفحل والمرعى زكيا كالواحد.

باب زكاة الحبوب والثمار

س٩٦: ما هي شروط وجوب زكاة الخارج من الأرض؟ وما مقدار نصابه؟ وما يجب فيه؟

ج: يشترط لوجوب زكاة الخارج من الأرض، من المكيل المدخر كالقمح والشعير، والثمر كالتمر والزبيب، شرطان:

الأول: أن يبلغ الخارج نصابا.

والثاني: أن يكون المزكى مالكا للنصاب وقت وجوبها.

ووقت الوجوب في الحب إذا اشتد، وفي الثمر إذا بدا صلاحها. والنصاب خمسة أوسق، وهي ثلاثمائة صاع شرعي. فإن سقي بلا كلفة ففيه العشر، وإن سقي بكلفة ففيه نصف العشر.

ويجب في العسل العشر، وأقل نصابه مائة وستون رطلا عراقيا.

وفي الركاز – وهو الكنز – يجب الخمس.

95. What is the niṣāb for goats and sheep? What is the ruling of mixed stock?

The minimum niṣāb for goats and sheep is forty and requires a Zakāt of one-year old sheep or six-month-old goat. For a hundred and twenty-one goats and sheep it is two sheep. For two hundred and one sheep and goats it is three sheep and for four hundred it is four sheep. And then for every one hundred sheep it is one sheep.

And if two or different herds (of different owners) are mixed together and they share the same space, pens, milking area, stud and pastures, then the Zakāt will be done as one.

Section on Zakāt of grains and fruit

96. What are the prerequisites that make Zakāt wājib for what is harvested? How much is its niṣāb and what is it's wājib amount?

There are two prerequisites for Zakāt to be wājib on harvest from the earth from that which is weighed by volume and stored such as wheat and barley or fruits such as dates and raisins. The first is that the harvest reaches niṣāb. The second is that the Zakāt payer has the niṣāb in his possession at the time of when it comes wājib.

The time of Zakāt becoming wājib is when the grains become firm and when the fruit ripens. Niṣāb is 5 awsaq[16] which is also 300 ṣāʿ.

If the land is watered without any exertion then Zakāt is ʿushr (one tenth). However, if water is supplied through irrigation then it will be half an ʿushr (or 1/20 or 5%). Zakāt of honey is ʿushr. The minimum niṣāb is a hundred and sixty Iraqi Riṭl (61.20 kg).
As for treasures (or anything mined) then 1/5th Zakāt is wājib.

[16] Five awsaq is approximately 613.05 Kg.

باب زكاة النقدين وعروض التجارة

س٩٧: كم هو نصاب الذهب والفضة، وكيف حكم عروض التجارة؟

ج: نصاب الذهب عشرون مثقالا، ونصاب الفضة مائتا درهم وفيهما ربع العشر.
ولا تجب الزكاة في حلي الذهب والفضة المباح المعد للاستعمال أو الإعارة.
ويشترط لوجوب الزكاة في عروض التجارة:

١. أن تبلغ نصابا بالذهب والفضة.
٢. وأن يحول عليها الحول عند صاحبها.

وتقوم عند تمام السنة وفيها ربع العشر.

باب زكاة الفطر

س٩٨: ما هي زكاة الفطر؟ وما حكمها؟

ج: زكاة الفطر صدقة، تجب للفطر من رمضان على كل:

١. مسلم.
٢. حر.
٣. يجد ما يفضل عن وقته وقوت عياله يوم العيد وليلته، بعدما يحتاج إليه من لوازمه الضرورية عن نفسه، وعمن يمونه من المسلمين.

Zakāt of gold, silver and merchandise

97. What is the niṣāb for gold and silver and what is the ruling of merchandise?

The niṣāb of gold is twenty mithqāl (or 85 grams) and the niṣāb of silver is two hundred dirhams (or 595 grams). The amount given is a quarter of a tenth (or 2.5%).

It is not wājib to give Zakāt for gold and silver permitted to use (for example gold is not allowed for men) which is prepared for personal usage or loaning.

The prerequisites for Zakāt to be wājib on merchandise are that it:

a. reaches the niṣāb value of gold or silver
b. a year passes on it in the possession of that person

It is payable at the end of the year and it is a quarter of a tenth (2.5%).

What is Zakātul Fiṭr?

98. What is Zakātul Fitr? What is its ruling?

Zakātul Fiṭr is ṣadaqa. It is wājib at the end of Ramaḍān upon:

a. every Muslim

b. free person

c. for the one that possesses beyond the daily bread for himself and his family for the day and night of ʿĪd and other than one needs for one self or that which is required for his Muslim dependants.

والأفضل إخراجها يوم العيد قبل الصلاة، وتكره بعدها، ويحرم تأخيرها عن يوم العيد، وتجوز قبله بيومين لا أكثر.

وهي صاع من تمر أو قمح أو زبيب أو شعير أو أقط - وهو اللبن المجمد - فإن لم توجد هذه الأصناف أخرجها من الذي يقتات به في البلد.

ولا يجزئ دفع قيمتها.

والصاع ستمائة وخمسة وثمانون درهما، وخمسة أسباع الدرهم.

باب أهل الزكاة

س٩٩: لمن تدفع الزكاة؟

ج: أهل الزكاة الذين تعطى لهم ثمانية، وهم:

١. الفقراء.
٢. والمساكين.
٣. والعاملون عليها - أي: المبعوثون لأخذها من أربابها.
٤. والمؤلفة قلوبهم.
٥. والمكاتبون.
٦. والغارمون.
٧. والغزاة.
٨. وابن السبيل - أي المنقطعون عن أوطانهم.

The best is to give it before the ʿīd ṣalāt on the day of ʿīd. It is makrūh afterwards. It is ḥarām to delay beyond the day of ʿīd. It can be given a day or two before.

It is a ṣāʿ of dates, wheat, raisins, barley or dried yoghurt. If these are not found then that which is customarily given in a land.

It is not permitted to give its value.

A ṣāʿ is 685 dirhams and 5/7 of a dirham (or 2.040 KG).

Chapter on recipients of Zakāt

99. Who should be given Zakāt?

The deserving recipients of zakāt are eight. They

are:

a. fuqarā or destitute

b. masākīn – the poor.

c. those who are appointed to work in collecting Zakāt.

d. those whose hearts needed to be inclined (e.g. leaders of a community whose acceptance of Islām is hoped or at least to protect Muslims from their evil)

e. slaves who have an agreement to buy their freedom

f. debtors

g. soldiers in the path of Allāh

h. travellers that are cut from his homeland (so he may get back home)

كتاب الحج

باب أحكام أهل الحج والعمرة

س١٠٠: ما حكم الحج والعمرة؟

ج: الحج والعمرة واجبان في العمر مرة،

بشروط خمسة، وهي:

١. الإسلام.
٢. والعقل.
٣. والبلوغ.
٤. وكمال الحرية.
٥. والاستطاعة.

ويصحان من الصغير والرقيق، ولا يجزآنهما عن حجة الإسلام.

فمن كملت فيه هذه الشروط لزمه السعي فورا، حيث كان في الطريق أمن.

والاستطاعة: هي القدرة على الزاد والراحلة، فاضلين عما يحتاجه لنفسه وعائلته على الدوام.

باب أركان الحج والعمرة

س١٠١: كم هي أركان الحج؟

ج: أركان الحج أربعة، وهي:

١. الإحرام – أي نية الدخول في النسك.

Chapter on Ḥaj
Section on the rulings of Ḥaj and ʿUmra

100. What are the rulings of Hajj and ʿUmra?

Hajj and ʿUmra are wājib once in a lifetime with the following five prerequisites:

a. Islām
b. soundness of mind
c. to have passed the age of puberty
d. to be completely free
e. ability

Ḥaj and ʿUmra will be acceptable from a minor or a slave. However, it will not be counted as fulfilling the compulsory obligation.

Anyone who has fulfilled the above five conditions, is then obliged to perform (Ḥaj and ʿUmra) immediately, as long as the journey getting there is safe.

Ability means that one has the provisions and transport for the journey and can provide for his family's needs until his return.

The arkān of Ḥaj and ʿUmra

101. How many arkān of Ḥaj are there?

There are four arkān of Ḥaj. They are:

a. Iḥrām i.e. intention to enter into the (Ḥaj/ʿUmra) rites

٢. والوقوف بعرفة، ووقته: من طلوع فجر التاسع من ذي الحجة إلى طلوع فجر عاشره.

٣. وطواف الإفاضة، وأول وقته من نصف ليلة العيد.

٤. والسعي بين الصفا والمروة.

س١٠٢: كم هي أركان العمرة؟

ج: أركان العمرة ثلاثة، وهي:

١. الإحرام.

٢. والطواف.

٣. والسعي.

باب واجبات الحج والعمرة

س١٠٣: كم هي واجبات الحج؟

ج: واجبات الحج سبعة، وهي:

١. الإحرام من الميقات.

٢. والوقوف بعرفة جزءا من الليل لمن وقف نهارا.

٣. والمبيت ليلة العيد بمزدلفة إلى نصف الليل لمن وافقها قبله.

٤. والمبيت بمنى ليالي أيام التشريق.

e. Wuqūf (literally standing, meaning staying) at ʿArafa. Its timing is from the start of Fajr of the ninth of Dhul Ḥijja until the start of Fajr of the tenth
f. Ṭawāful Ifāḍa (of the Kaʿbā). It starts from midnight of the eve of ʿĪd
g. Saʿī (walking) between Ṣafā and Marwa

102. How many arkān does ʿUmra have?

ʿUmra has three arkān. They are:

a. Iḥrām
b. Ṭawāf
c. Saʿī

Wājib acts of Ḥaj and Umrah

103. How many wājib acts are there in Ḥaj?

There are seven wājib acts of Ḥaj. They are:

a. iḥrām from the Mīqāt (boundary of the holy sanctuary)
b. Wuqūf at ʿArafa for part of the night if one stayed there in the day
c. staying in Muzdalifa on the eve of ʿĪd till midnight for those who stayed there before midnight.
d. spending the nights of tashrīq at Mina

٥. ورمي الجمار مرتبا – بأن يرمي يوم العيد جمرة العقبة التي تلي مكة، وفي اليوم الثاني وما بعده يرمي أولا الجمرة التي تلي مسجد الخيف، ثم الوسطى، ثم العقبة، كل واحدة بسبع حصيات تصيب المرمى.
٦. والحلق أو التقصير.
٧. وطواف الوداع.

س١٠٤: كم هي واجبات العمرة؟

ج: واجبات العمرة هي:
١. الإحرام لها من خارج الحرم.
٢. والحلق أو التقصير.

باب محظورات الإحرام

س١٠٥ : ما الذي يحرم على المحرم فعله؟

ج: يحرم على المحرم:
١. تعمد لبس المخيط على الرجل، وتعمد تغطية الوجه من الأنثى، والرأس من الرجل.
٢. وقصد شم الطيب ومسه، واستعماله في نحو أكل وشرب.
٣. وإزالة الشعر عن جميع البدن.
٤. وتقليم الأظفار.

e. stoning at the Jamarāt in order: on the day of ʿĪd (tenth) to stone the Jamratul ʿAqaba which is closest to Makka, on the second day (eleventh) and in all subsequent days, one stones the first Jamra near masjid Khīf, then the central one and then Jamratul ʿAqaba. Every jamra is stoned with seven stones that should reach the Jamra
f. shave or trim hair
g. farewell Tawāf

104. How many wājibs of ʿumra are there?

Wājibs of ʿumra are:

a. iḥrām for ʿumra from outside of the Ḥaram
b. shaving or trimming hair

Section on restrictions of Ḥaj

105. What is ḥarām for the muḥrim (one in ihram)?

For the muḥrim it is ḥarām:

a. to intentionally wear stitched garment for men, intentionally cover the face for a woman and also the head for the men
b. intend to smell perfume or touch it, to consume it in food and drink
c. removing hair from the body
d. clipping nails

٥. وقتل صيد البر، والدلالة عليه، والإعانة على قتله.
٦. وعقد النكاح.
٧. والوطء في الفرج، ودواعيه، والمباشرة دون الفرج، والاستمناء.

س١٠٦: ما يجب على من فعل شيئًا من هذه المحرمات؟

ج: يجب على من لبس، أو تطيب، أو غطى رأسه، أو أزال أكثر من شعرتين، أو ظفرين: ذبح شاة، أو صيام ثلاثة أيام، أو إطعام ستة مساكين مما يجزئ من الفطرة.

ويجب على من أتلف صيدا له مثل من النعم ذبح مثله، أو تقديم ذلك المثل عن محل الإتلاف أو ما قاربه، ويشتري بقيمته طعاما يجزئ من الفطرة، فيطعم كل مسكين مدا من القمح، أو يصوم عن طعام كل مسكين يوما.

وما لا مثل له يضمن بالقيمة.

والحمد لله على التمام، والصلاة والسلام على خير الأنام، وعلى آله وأصحابه الأعلام، وأرزقنا بجاههم حسن الختام.

آمين.

جمعت بقلم الفقير موسى القَدُّومي غفر الله له ولوالديه.

آمين.

e. hunting or pointing out a hunt or assisting in killing it

f. marriage contract

g. sexual intercourse, that which leads up to intercourse, foreplay and masturbation

106. What is the penalty for one who does any of the above?

It is wājib for one who wears clothing (as in 105 b), perfumes his body, covers his head, removes more than two hairs or two nails: to slaughter a sheep or fast for three days, or feed six poor people the amount of Ṣadaqatul Fiṭr.

It is wājib on one who hunt and kills prey the size of cattle (sheep, camel or cow) to slaughter something of a similar size i.e. the slaughtered animal will take place of the hunted animal and should be the same size or approximately the same size. One may alternatively purchase food of the same value that would be in accordance to Ṣadaqatul Fiṭr i.e. feed every poor person a mudd of wheat or alternatively, one may fast one day for the number of each poor person.

If one does not have an equivalent animal then its value can be paid as compensation.

All Praise is due to Allāh upon this completion. And peace and blessings be on the best of creation and upon his family and companions and provide by their rank, a good ending. Āmīn.

This (book) was gathered by the pen of the faqīr Musa Quddūmi. May Allāh forgive him and his parents. Āmīn.

Appendices

The Ḥanbali madhhab is one of the four canonical schools of jurisprudence considered to be reliable among Muslims; from its inception it has been attributed to the great imām, faqīh and muḥaddith Imām Aḥmad bin Ḥanbal Ash-Shaybāni. He became renowned for his reverence of the Prophetic narrations and the sayings of the Ṣaḥāba and based his fiqh upon these. When one reflects upon his prodigal memory, the immensity of his knowledge and his countless shaykhs, one realises that, in his era, there was none like him, as was recognised by his contemporaries far and wide.

As an introduction to Imām Aḥmad bin Ḥanbal and some of the inner workings of the Ḥanbali madhhab, these appendices have been added. The Ḥanbali madhhab section was extracted and translated from a booklet on the founding imams, stages of development and principles of the four madhhabs prepared by the Darul Iftā's Research Unit of the Kuwaiti Awqāf Ministry. The Ḥanbali section was reviewed by Shaykh ʿAdnān bin Sālim An-Nahhām,[17] who wrote: "I have reviewed this introduction on

[17] Shaykh ʿAdnān bin Sālim An-Nahhām is the foremost student of the late great scholar and jurist of Kuwait, Shaykh Muḥammad bin Sulaymān Jarrāḥ. Shaykh ʿAdnān took over as the Imām at Shaykh Jarrāḥ's masjid after Shaykh Jarrāḥ's demise. Shaykh ʿAdnān has taught (and at the time of publication continues to teach) there the books of the Ḥanbalis such as Dalīlut Tālib, Akhṣarul Mukhtaṣarāt, Rawdul Murbiʿ etc. His classes are well known and well attended by seekers and ʿulamā from all over Kuwait as he is recognised as an authority in the madhhab. He also has written Hāshiyas or glosses on some books of the madhhab such as Akhṣarul Mukhtaṣarāt of Ibn Balbān, Muntahā Irādāt and its Sharḥ by Buhūti and on some books of Naḥw such as Qatrun Nadā of Ibn Hishām and Sharḥ Ibn ʿAqīl (which is presently incomplete). Unfortunately, at this point in time, none of these works have been published.

Ḥanbali fiqh by the Research Unit. It contains Imām Aḥmad's biography, a summary of his method of deriving rulings upon which our companions (Ḥanbali imāms) base their actions. It is in accordance with the books of uṣūl such as Tahrīr and Kawkabul Munīr and their commentaries. Also, it is in accordance with important texts of the madhhab like Muntahā and Iqnā', upon which the fatwas of the Muta-akhkhirīn (latter-era Ḥanbalis) are based."

The following subjects are covered:

1. Biography of Imām Aḥmad bin Ḥanbal
2. Stages of development of the madhhab
3. General principles of deriving rulings in the madhhab
4. The most well-known works within the madhhab
5. The terminology used in the madhhab

Appendix 1: Biography of Imām Aḥmad bin Ḥanbal

Name and lineage

He was known as Abu ʿAbdullah; Aḥmad bin Muḥammad bin Ḥanbal bin Hilāl bin Asad Ash-Shaybāni Al-Marwazi Al-Baṣri by paternal lineage. He was born and brought up in Baghdād. His family tree meets with the Prophet's ﷺ at Nizār bin Maʿd bin ʿAdnān.

As for his mother, she was from the Banu ʿĀmir clan of the Shaybān tribe. Her name was Ṣafiyya.[18]

Birth and upbringing

Imām Aḥmad bin Ḥanbal was born in Baghdād in the month of Rabiʾul Awwal, 163 AH. His mother arrived in Baghdād from Merv when she was expecting him. His father was a soldier who was stationed at Merv and was transferred to Baghdād. However, his father passed away at the age of thirty, when Imām Aḥmad was only three years old and was therefore brought up by his mother. She dutifully paid attention to his moral upbringing and raised him in an atmosphere of piety and knowledge. She would diligently send him to the maktab. He continued in this way until he excelled his peers. Due to the family's poverty, the teacher would sometimes not take fees but would instead take assistance from Imām Aḥmad in teaching the other children. He was exceptional among the youth of his generation in piety and his

[18] Sīratul Imām Aḥmad bin Ḥanbal, Ṣāliḥ bin Aḥmad, p. 30; Tarīkh Baghdād, Khatīb Baghdādi, vol. 4, p. 412; Manāqibul Imām Aḥmad, Ibn Jawzī, pp. 16-21; Siyaru Aʿlāmun Nubalā, Dhahabi, vol. 11, pp 177-179; Al-Maqṣadul Arshad fi Dhikril Imām Aḥmad, Burhān Ibn Mufliḥ, vol. 1, p. 64.

speech was pure and morally excellent.[19]

Seeking knowledge

From an early age, Imām Aḥmad had an intense love for seeking knowledge of dīn. He was diligent and hardworking in his studies. Students used to come from all over the world to study in Baghdād. When he was seventeen, he started his travels in the acquisition of knowledge. His travels took him to Kūfa, Baṣra, Makkah, Madīnah, Yemen, Shām and throughout the Arabian Peninsula. He documented knowledge from the scholars of all these lands.

His desire for knowledge was so much that he always arrived at the gatherings of knowledge and ḥadīth classes before fajr. His mother would hold him by his clothes to stop him leaving home so early. She would say to him, "Not until the athān is given."[20] He studied so diligently that he could not get an opportunity to earn a livelihood or get married. He only married when he reached the age of forty, after he had satiated his thirst for knowledge.[21]

Imām Aḥmad's initial studies were in seeking the knowledge of ḥadīth. He started with Hushaym ibn Bashīr and, out of all of his teachers, he spent the longest time with him; that is, from 179 AH until 183 AH. He also wrote aḥādīth from Qāḍi Abu Yūsuf, the student of Imām Abu Ḥanīfa. He also learnt from ʿAbdur Raḥmān bin Mahdi and Abu Bakr bin ʿAyyash.[22] May Allāh fill all their graves with nūr.

Even when he was older, his age and vast knowledge didn't prevent him from attending and continuing gatherings of

---

[19] Tarīkh Baghdād, vol. 4, p. 415; Manāqibul Imām Aḥmad, pp. 22-44; Tahdhībul Kamāl, Mizzi, vol. 1, p. 445; Siyaru Aʿlāmun Nubalā, Dhahabi, vol. 11, p. 179; Mafātīḥul Fiqhul Ḥanbali, Sālim Ath-Thaqafi, vol. 1, p. 127.

[20] Manāqibul Imām Aḥmad, p. 37.

[21] Sīratul Imām Aḥmad bin Ḥanbal, pp. 31-33; Manāqibul Imām Aḥmad, p. 72; Tahdhībul Kamāl, vol. 1, p. 437; Siyaru Aʿlāmun Nubalā, vol. 11, p. 185.

[22] Sīratul Imām Aḥmad bin Ḥanbal, p. 31; Tarīkh Baghdād, vol. 4, p. 416; Manāqibul Imām Aḥmad, pp. 26,37.

knowledge attended by much younger seekers. He used to listen and write the lessons without being bored or fatigued. Someone saw him at this age with an ink-pot and remarked, "O Abu ʿAbdullah! You are still like this (i.e. studying knowledge) and you are an imām of the Muslims!" Imām Aḥmad replied: "with the ink-pot until the grave." He also used to say, "I will seek knowledge until I enter the grave."[23]

His most well-known teachers

Imām Aḥmad obtained knowledge from many teachers, specifically Imāms of ḥadīth and fiqh and other Islamic sciences. However, he was more inclined to the science of transmission of ḥadīth, as he saw in this the veneration of the sunna of the Prophet ﷺ. The number of his teachers reached four hundred and fourteen men and one woman.[24] The most famous of these were:

1. Imām Abu Yūsuf or Yaʿqūb bin Ibrāhīm (d. 182 AH), the well-known chief justice of the khalīfa, Harūn Rashīd
2. Hushaym bin Bashīr (d. 183 AH)
3. Ismāʿīl bin ʿUlayya (d. 193 AH)
4. Wakīʿ bin Jarraḥ (d. 197 AH)
5. Sufyān bin ʿUyaina (d. 198 AH)
6. Abu Dawūd Aṭ-Ṭayālasi (d. 204 AH)
7. Muḥammad bin Idrīs Ash Shāfiʿī (d. 204 AH)
8. ʿAbdur Razzaq bin Hammām Aṣ-Ṣanʿāni (d. 211 AH)
9. Nuʿaym bin Ḥammād (d. 228 AH)

[23] Manāqibul Imām Aḥmad, p. 37.
[24] Manāqibul Imām Aḥmad, pp. 40-67.

10. Yaḥya bin Maʿīn (d. 233 AH)

11. Ishāq bin Ibrāhīm bin Rāhawayh (d. 238 AH)[25]

May Allāh taʿāla be pleased with all of them.

His most well-known pupils

Imām Aḥmad's fame spread throughout the Muslim world. He was sought out by students from everywhere. His gatherings were well attended and five hundred and seventy-seven gained expertise in fiqh under him. Apart from these, thousands of unnamed people attended his gatherings to derive benefit. Even many of his own teachers used to sit in his gatherings. Many biographers have recorded that a single gathering was attended by more than five thousand people who observed the highest form of adab.[26] His most well-known students were Wakīʿ bin Jarraḥ (d. 197 AH), Abu ʿUbayd Al-Qāsim bin Sallam (d. 224 AH), Yaḥya bin Maʿīn (d. 233 AH), Ishāq bin Ibrāhīm bin Rāhawayh (d. 238 AH), Muḥammad bin Ismāʿīl Al-Bukhāri (d. 256 AH), Aḥmad bin Muḥammad bin Hāni Aṭ-Ṭai or else known as Abu Bakr Al-Athram (d. 261 AH), Muslim bin Hajjāj Nisāpūri (d. 261 AH), ʿUbaydullah bin ʿAbdul Karīm or Abu Zurʿa Ar-Rāzi (d. 264 AH), Ṣāliḥ bin Aḥmad bin Ḥanbal (d. 266 AH), Ḥanbal bin Ishāq bin Ḥanbal (d. 273 AH), ʿAbdul Malik bin ʿAbdul Ḥamīd Al-Maymūni (d. 274 AH), Ishāq bin Ibrāhīm bin Hāni Nisāpūri (d. 275 AH), Sulaymān bin Al-Ashʿath Abu Dawūd As-Sijistāni (d. 275 AH), Ḥarb bin Ismāʿīl Al-Karmāni (d. 280 AH), ʿAbdullah bin Aḥmad bin Ḥanbal (d. 290 AH), Muhannā bin Yaḥya Ash-Shāmi and many more.[27]

His knowledge and fiqh

Imām Aḥmad bin Ḥanbal was an imām in ḥadīth and the Sunna. He

---

[25] Manāqibul Imām Aḥmad, pp. 40 onwards; Tahdhībul Kamāl, vol. 1, pp. 437 onwards.

[26] Manāqibul Imām Aḥmad, p. 77.

[27] Manāqibul Imām Aḥmad, pp. 107 onwards; Tahdhībul Kamāl, vol. 1, pp. 440 onwards.

was renowned for this science more than any other Islāmic science. However, the reality is that he had combined between transmission of ḥadīth narrations and a deep study of its contents. He was an imām in fiqh and possessed a deep understanding of it. When he spoke on fiqh, he had critically analysed all the sciences and knowledge and spoke with profound and deep understanding.[28]

When one reflects on the life of Imām Aḥmad and that, at the beginning of his life, he was a student of Qāḍi Abu Yūsuf (the student of Imām Abu Ḥanīfa) and at the end of his life he was a student of Imām Shāfiʿī, one realises that Imām Aḥmad spent a considerable portion of his life in the acquisition of the science of fiqh and attained depth in his knowledge. Abu Qāsim Al-Jubali stated that "whenever, Imām Aḥmad bin Ḥanbal was asked regarding any issue, it was as though the knowledge of the whole world was before him."[29]

Ibrāhīm Al-Ḥarbi said that "when I saw Imām Aḥmad bin Ḥanbal; it was as though that Allāh had blessed him with all types of knowledge of all eras and generations. He used to speak from it what he wished and left what he wished." [30]

Aḥmad bin Saʿīd Ad-Dārimy said that "I have not seen someone with a blacker head (of hair - referring to his youth), who had memorised aḥādīth of the Messenger of Allāh ﷺ and of its fiqh and was knowledgeable of its meanings more so than Abu ʿAbdullah Aḥmad bin Ḥanbal."[31]

From the vastness of his knowledge and understanding was that

---

[28] Al-Madkhal ilā Madhhabil Imām Aḥmad bin Ḥanbal, Ibn Badrān, p. 45.

[29] Manāqibul Imām Aḥmad, p. 77; Tabaqāt Shāfiʿiyya Al-Kubrā, Subkī, vol. 2, p. 28.

[30] Tadhkiratul Huffaẓ, Dhahabi, vol. 2, p. 16; Ṭabaqāt Shāfiʿiyya Al-Kubrā, vol. 2, p. 28.

[31] Tarīkh Baghdād, vol. 4, p. 419; Manāqibul Imām Aḥmad, p. 78.

he became a reference for others and had intimate knowledge on the methods and jurisprudence of other madhhabs and knew the finer points of their schools. Ibn Taymiyya mentioned that Imām Aḥmad bin Ḥanbal and Aḥmad bin Faraj (Ibn Jawzī) used to both be asked about the masāil (jurisprudence issues) related to Imām Mālik's, Imām Sufyān Thawri's, Imām Al-Awzā'ī's and Imām Abu Ḥanīfa madhhabs."[32]

Many great Imāms acknowledged Imām Aḥmad's acumen in, fiqh such as 'Abdur Razzāq Aṣ-Ṣan'āni, Abu 'Ubayd Qāsim bin Sallam, Abu Thawr, Imām Shāfi'ī, 'Alī bin Madīnī, Ibn Wārah, Nasāi, Sāliḥ bin Muḥammad Jazarah, Al-Būshanjī, Abu Zur'a` Rāzi, Ishāq bin Rāhawayh, Abu Ḥatim Rāzi, Yaḥya bin Ma'īn, and many more.[33]

Imām Aḥmad and Imām Shāfi'ī were contemporaries, whose association lasted over forty years and he benefited from Imām Shāfi'ī's fiqh and knowledge. Imām Shāfi'ī travelled to Baghdād twice and both times Imām Aḥmad studied with him. Imām Aḥmad also met him on his journey to Makkah. His shaykh, Imām Shāfi'ī, bore witness to Imām Aḥmad as an Imām (leader) in fiqh and knowledge. He said "Aḥmad is an Imām in regard to eight characteristics: Imām in ḥadīth, Imām in fiqh, Imām in lughah (Arabic language), Imām in Qurān, Imām in faqr (pious self-sufficiency), Imām in asceticism, Imām in piety and Imām in sunna."[34]

Imām Ishāq bin Rāhawayh too had a long-standing friendship with Imām Aḥmad. They both travelled together seeking knowledge and revised their lessons together.[35] Ibn Taymiyyah said "there is more agreement between Imām Aḥmad, Imām Shāfi'ī and Ishāq than between other scholars of their calibre. Imām Aḥmad's principles are their principles. Imām Aḥmad praised and honoured them. His school is based heavily on the principles of the fuqahā

---

[32] Majmu'āl Fatāwa, Ibn Taymiyya, vol. 34, p. 114.

[33] Siyarul A'lāmun Nubalā, vol. 11, pp. 195-203.

[34] Ṭabaqātul Ḥanābila, Abu Ya'lā, vol. 1, p. 3.

[35] Siyaru A'lāmun Nubalā, vol. 11, pp 188, 193; Al-Madkhal Al-Mufaṣṣal ilā Fiqhil Imām Aḥmad bin Ḥanbal, Bakr Abu Zayd, vol. 1, pp. 269, 270.

(or jurists) of ḥadīth and thus he considered them superior to others. Imām Shāfi'ī and Ishāq were considered to be among the greatest jurists of their era.[36] Their influence on Imām Aḥmad is apparent, as he strictly adhered to the overall ḥadīth-derived fiqh methodology. If any matter came up, he would first refer to the Qurān, then the Sunna and then the sayings of the Saḥāba and narrations about them. As for qiyās or analogy, it was subsidiary and of secondary importance to the first three which were considered absolute sources of dīn. This can clearly be seen from the fatwas that were given by Imām Aḥmad.

Shaykh Muḥammed Abu Zuhra said "Imām Aḥmad was an authority in ḥadīth. Through this authority he was an authority in fiqh. In fact, his fiqh, speech, comparisons, expressions and explanations in his opinions and fatwas on various issues show that he was a jurist who based everything on the direct text of the aḥādīth and companions' narrations."[37]

Imām Aḥmad's fiqhi uniqueness and genius was that he had numerous independent positions on many fiqh issues which are narrated in the books of the madhhab as answers to questions that were posed to him by his students. The books of these students on fiqh, the reasoning behind the rulings, proofs for the positions taken and the individual deep insight into the issues and how these rulings were derived are recorded.[38]

Imām Aḥmad's Works

Imām Aḥmad is famous for his extensive authored works which indicate his extensive knowledge, collections of numerous

---

[36] Majmu'āl Fatāwa, vol. 34, p. 113.

[37] Ibn Ḥanbal, Abu Zuhra, pp. 154-155.

[38] Muqaddima of the Masāil Imām Aḥmad on the riwāyah of 'Abdullah, 'Ali Al-Muhanna, vol. 1, p. 28; Al-Madkhal Al-Mufaṣṣal ilā Fiqhil Imām Aḥmad bin Ḥanbal, vol. 1, pp. 371, 373.

Prophetic narrations and deep understanding. There are nearly thirty works attributed to him and nearly two hundred books written by his students which are compilations of his answers to questions. These works collectively cover the entirety of religious sciences including ʿAqīda, Qurān and its sciences, ḥadīth and its sciences and Fiqh. Some of these works are:

- Al-Musnad – This is really his greatest work in size and status, as it is a compilation of forty thousand aḥādīth
- Faḍāilus Ṣaḥāba – On the virtues of ṣaḥāba
- Al-ʿilal wal Maʿrifatur Rijāl
- Al-Asāmi wal Kunā
- Ar-raddu ʿalā Zanādiqa wal Jahmiyyah
- An Nāsikh wal Mansūkh
- Al-Muqaddam wal Muakhkhar Fil Qurān
- Al-Manāsik
- Al-Kabīr wal Ṣaghīr[39]

Praises of Imām Aḥmad by the ʿulamā

Imām Aḥmad was the embodiment of deep knowledge, perfect manners, lofty character and trustworthiness in knowledge until he surpassed all his peers and was a proof of Allāh Taʿāla to the creation. His contemporaries acknowledged and praised him extensively:

1. Imām Shāfiʿī said "I left Baghdād. But I did not leave behind someone more pious, God-fearing, with a more deeper understanding and knowledge than Aḥmad bin Ḥanbal."[40]

---

[39] Al-Madkhal ilā Madhhabil Imām Aḥmad bin Ḥanbal, vol. 1, p. 44; Al-Madkhal Al-Mufaṣṣal ilā Fiqhil Imām Aḥmad bin Ḥanbal, vol. 1, pp. 352-354.

[40] Tarīkh Baghdād, vol. 4, p. 419; Tadhkiratul Huffaẓ, vol. 2, p. 16.

2. ʿAli bin Madīnī said "I have taken Aḥmad bin Ḥanbal as an Imām between me and Allāh (i.e. I refer to him in matters of dīn). People will be on a firm standing if they base their dīn on what Abu ʿAbdullah has based it on."[41]

3. Abu ʿUbayd Al-Qāsim bin Sallam said "knowledge culminates in four: Aḥmad bin Ḥanbal, who has the deepest understanding; ʿAli bin Madīnī, who is the most knowledgeable; Yaḥya bin Maʿīn, who wrote the most; and Ibn Abi Shaybah, who memorised the most."[42]

4. Yaḥya bin Maʿīn said "people want to be like Aḥmad bin Ḥanbal. I will never be able to be like him."[43]

5. Bishr bin Al-Hārith Al-Ḥāfi was asked once about Aḥmad bin Ḥanbal. He said "I have been asked about Imām Aḥmad bin Ḥanbal! He entered a furnace and came out pure gold."[44]

6. Abu Zurʿa Ar-Rāzi said "my eyes did not see the likes of Aḥmad bin Ḥanbal." ʿAbdullah bin Muḥammad bin Abdul Karīm asked "in regard to knowledge?" He said, "in knowledge, in zuhd (abstinence), in fiqh, in maʿrifat (cognisance) and in all good my eyes did not see the likes of him."[45]

The greatest incident in his life that tells us of his status, virtue, steadfastness and how he surpassed all others was his patience and firm-footedness in the days of 'the Great Trial' or *Miḥna.* It began during the rule of the Abbāsi khalīfa Mamūn and continued until

---

[41] Al-Majrūḥīn, Ibn Ḥibbān, vol. 1, p. 56; Tarīkh Dimashq, Ibn ʿAsākir, vol. 5, p. 279.

[42] Al-Jarḥ wa Taʿdīl, Ibn Abi Hātim, vol. 1, p. 293; Tadhkiratul Huffaẓ, vol. 2, p. 17.

[43] Al-Jarḥ wa Taʿdīl, vol. 1, p. 298; Siyaru Aʿlāmun Nubalā, vol. 11, p 197.

[44] Siyaru Aʿlāmun Nubalā, vol. 11, p 197; Tahdhībul Kamāl, vol. 1, p. 454.

[45] Manāqibul Imām Aḥmad, p. 163.

the era of Muʿtaṣim and Al-Wāthiq. They insisted on the transience of the Qurān, that the Qurān is created and not an eternal attribute of Allāh Taʿāla as was always known and believed by Muslims. Imām Aḥmad stood firmly against the false doctrine and upheld the truth as firmly as a mountain. He refused to comply and compromise under pressure from the authorities. He underwent torture and imprisonment for those beliefs and through him the beliefs of the Muslims were saved. This continued until the khalīfa Mutawakkil ascended the throne and gave up the false doctrine and aided the Ahlus Sunna.[46]

His death

Imām Aḥmad passed away in Baghdād, midmorning on the day of Jumuʿa on the 12th of Rabiʿ ul Awwal in the year 241 AH. He was seventy-seven years old. He was buried after ʿaṣr. He had a fever from the Wednesday of the previous week, so he was ill for nine days. His condition worsened over that period and he did not recover. His janāza was attended by such a large crowd, which was never seen by Muslims before.[47] May Allāh Taʿāla descend His special mercy on Imām Aḥmad. May he be blessed with the highest levels of Firdaws.

---

[46] See the details of the *Miḥna* or *Great Trial* in regards to the non-createdness of the Qurān in: Manāqibul Imām Aḥmad, p. 416 onwards; Siyaru Aʿlāmun Nubalā, vol. 11, p. 236 onwards.

[47] Tarīkh Baghdād, vol. 4, p. 422; Al-Maqṣadul Arshad fi Dhikril Imām Aḥmad, vol. 1, p. 70.

Appendix 2 - Historical development[48] & stages of the Ḥanbali school

There is no school of thought in the history of sharīʿa sciences except that it went through numerous stages in its development. Only through the passage of time can a school truly reveal the intricacies of its methodology, legal theory and philosophy (uṣūl and qawāʾid) and the manner in which the school derived ruling based on these. To achieve this, ʿulamā adopted the science of fiqh and teaching of the rulings of fiqh. They spread this science and authored works on it, to the point where seekers of knowledge held fiqh in high esteem and strived to attain understanding in it and its principles. The development of the Ḥanbali school can be divided in to four broad stages.

1st Stage: Inception and foundation: 204 - 241 AH

This stage began in 204 AH, as this was the year that Imām Aḥmad started teaching and issuing fatwa. He was forty years old. Prior to this phase, he focused on studying and acquiring knowledge. He strengthened his position in the Islāmic sciences and sharpened his juristic abilities.[49]

If one looks at the intellectual development of Imām Aḥmad, then it can be appreciated how he arrived at the principles of the Ḥanbali school. He sought knowledge from a vast number of scholars in all the primary Islāmic sciences and secondary sciences

---

[48] **Note:** *Development* of a madhhab and its related historical phases should be understood as discovering and systemising the works of the founding mujtahid by the scholars of each era. It should not be misconstrued as modifications of the madhhab by others. Some modern thinkers misunderstand the stages as changes to the madhhab. In reality, they are not changes, but an appreciation and a 'going back to' the founding mujtahid of the madhhab. Current contexts, social and political pressure are a later consideration. They don't drive the madhhab, let alone change it.

[49] Mafātīḥul Fiqhul Ḥanbali, vol. 1, pp. 160, 162.

as well.

Imām Aḥmad developed an acumen in the memorisation of ḥadīth narrations and rulings of fiqh, until seekers of knowledge started noticing him. They then started to attend his gatherings, recorded his lectures, sought clarifications and fatwas from him. Accordingly, his knowledge become well-known among the masses. His students were aided in their understanding through his sayings, personal actions and writings on various issues related to ʿaqīda, uṣūl, ḥadīth and fiqh. These were produced by him personally or under his direct supervision. They totalled nearly two hundred works.[50]

2nd Stage: Transmission and growth: 241 – 403 AH

This stage is considered an extension of the first stage. The students of Imām Aḥmad transmitted the madhhab to their own students and beyond via lectures, authored works and correspondence. Imām Khallāl noted regarding Sāliḥ (d. 266 AH), the son of Imām Aḥmad "that people used to write to him from Khorasān and other places and that he used to write to them and answer their masāil faultlessly (based on Imām Aḥmad's principles)."[51]

Ibn Abi Ḥatim said "ʿAbdullah (son of Imām Aḥmad) wrote to me (on fiqhi issues) based on the masāil of his father along with the reasonings derived from aḥādīth."[52] ʿAbdullah had gathered his father's masāil in fiqh and had arranged them according to topics.[53]

Among Imām Aḥmad's students who had systematically recorded fiqhi masāil narrated from his teacher was Muḥammad bin Ḥatim

---

[50] Al-Madkhal Al-Mufaṣṣal ilā Fiqhil Imām Aḥmad bin Ḥanbal, vol. 1, pp. 133, 134.

[51] Ṭabaqātul Ḥanābila, vol. 1, p. 172.

[52] Al-Jarḥ wa Taʿdīl, vol. 5, p. 7

[53] Mafātīḥul Fiqhul Ḥanbali, vol. 2, pp. 367.

Aṭ-Ṭayy Al-Athram (d. 261 AH).[54]

Aḥmad Ibn Al-Khuṣayb bin ʿAbdur Raḥmān was another student of Imām Aḥmad who was known for his lectures and classes. He was well-known in Tarsus. He held fiqh-specific classes. Imām Khallāl noted that he transmitted masāil from Imām Aḥmad meticulously.[55]

Imām Khallāl narrates regarding the era of Imām Aḥmad's students and their promoting and spreading of his fiqh in these words: "Abu Bakr Al-Marwazi went out to participate in a battle. He was escorted by people to Samarra (military headquarters of the Abbasids). He tried to send them off, but they would not leave. Many left him. But the ones that remained were about fifty thousand in number. It was said to him "O Abu Bakr, praise Allāh, this knowledge is spreading due to you". He wept and said that 'this knowledge is not mine. This is the knowledge of none other than Aḥmad bin Ḥanbal'."[56]

The above is sufficient proof of the transmission of the fiqh and knowledge of Imām Aḥmad by his students directly from him. There was such a large number of students from whom Imām Khallāl narrated in his unique encyclopedia and magnus corpus "Al-Jāmiʿ li ʿulūm Imām Aḥmad." Imām Khallāl had the good fortune of studying under a large number of Imām Aḥmad's students who all recorded and narrated from their teacher.

Other ways in which the school of Imām Aḥmad was transmitted include that many of his students were appointed to influential positions as qāḍīs. These qāḍīs judged according to the teachings of Imām Aḥmad. From the well-known judges were:

1. Imām Aḥmad's son Sāliḥ (d. 266 AH). He was appointed in

---

[54] Ṭabaqātul Ḥanābila, vol. 1, p. 66.
[55] Ṭabaqātul Ḥanābila, vol. 1, p. 42.
[56] Ṭabaqātul Ḥanābila, vol. 1, p. 56.

Tarsus and Esfahan.[57]

2. Al-Ḥasan bin Mūsa Al-Ashyab (d. 209 AH). He was a judge in Mosul, Homs and Tabaristan.[58]

The second generation of the students i.e. Imām Aḥmad's students' students recorded the masāil directly from their teachers and busied themselves in gathering, recording, organising and classifying the masāil. This phase was known as the "era of the Mutaqaddimīn" or the early authorities in the school" and this ended with the passing away of Al-Ḥasan bin Ḥāmid in 403 AH.

This period was critical and the ʿulamā that became proficient in the methodology and school of Imām Aḥmad had the far-reaching impact in the establishment and propagation of the still nascent school. The most outstanding figure of this phase was the aforementioned Imām Aḥmad bin Muḥammad Al-Khallāl (d. 311 AH). He would travel, sit with and write from all of Imām Aḥmad's students in regards to all aspects of his methodology of fiqh and masāil derived thereby. He gathered all of these in Al-Jāmiʿ. It was after this book that ʿulamā would identify themselves with the madhhab of Imām Aḥmad. As many ʿulamā became experts in the school, works started to appear in the madhhab. Al-Jāmiʿ became a reference for all those works afterwards, for students and scholars alike.

Also, in this phase, ʿulamā began working on more shorter treatises (mutūn) and basic compendiums on the masāil of the madhhab. Abu Qāsim ʿUmar bin Ḥusayn Al-Khiraqi (d. 334 AH) was the first in this generation and became well-known as he produced the first matn-text in the madhhab (structured on the traditional order of a fiqh book). It is known as "Mukhtaṣarul Khiraqi."

Also, among this generation was Abu Bakr ʿAbdul ʿAzīz bin Jaʿfar better - known as the slave of Al-Khallāl. He died in 363 AH. He laboured over the work of Imām Khallāl with a deep and thorough study and then elucidated its contents and presented it

[57] Ṭabaqātul Ḥanābila, vol. 1, p. 175.
[58] Ṭabaqātul Ḥanābila, vol. 1, p. 138.

comprehensively and provided the most correct view of Imām Aḥmad where there was a difference.

The recording of the masāil did not end at Imām Khallāl - Al-Ḥasan bin Ḥāmid (d. 403 AH) authored "Al-Jāmiʿ fil Madhhab" in 400 chapters (approximately 20 volumes). He arranged it according to the traditional fiqh structure.

Furthermore, in this phase ʿulamā wrote mutūn on the soundest opinion regarding issues, where there might be contradictory opinions transmitted from Imām Aḥmad e.g. the book "An-Nasīha" by Abu Bakr Al-Ājurri (d. 360 AH) or mutūn that recorded two opinions on issues like Kitābul Qawlayn of ʿAbdul ʿAzīz Ghulām Khallāl. Also, small treatises or epistles were written discussing individual masāil or topics e.g. "Al-Manāsik" by Ibn Baṭṭa Al-ʿUkburi (d. 387 AH).

Lastly, this phase also produced works on the underlying workings and philosophy of the madhhab i.e. uṣūl of fiqh or principles of jurisprudence and its related terminology, as was done by Al-Ḥasan bin Ḥāmid in his books "Uṣūlul Fiqh" and "Tahdhībul Ajwiba".[59]

3rd Stage: Refinement, revision and text preparation: 403 – 884 AH

This stage starts from the fifth century and continued until the end of the ninth century. It started after the passing away of Al-Ḥasan bin Ḥāmid (d. 403 AH) until the passing away of Al-Burhan bin Mufliḥ (d. 884 AH). Once the masāil had crystallised, the need arose to revise, refine and put into easily available books which were according to standard fiqh texts.

This era is referred as to the "era of the mutawasiṭṭīn" or the

[59] Al-Madkhal Al-Mufaṣṣal ilā Fiqhil Imām Aḥmad bin Ḥanbal, vol. 1, pp. 133, 134; Muqaddima of Al-Jāmiʿ li ʿUlūmil Imām Aḥmad, Khalid Rabbāṭ & Sayyid ʿĪd, vol. 1, p.89.

"middle-era authorities in the school". The mutawasiṭṭīn developed maxims and principles of understanding how the masāil of Imām Aḥmad are to be applied. They established principles whereby the masāil can be understood in terms of how they were derived from the sources and to give preference to Imām Aḥmad's strongest narration or opinion on an issue (if there are conflicting narrations from the Imām). They finalised the uṣūl of the fiqh of Imām Aḥmad. This required a deep study of all the masāil and involved the search for underlying maxims or principles that govern groupings of masāil of the Imām. The school had a rich resource of the mujtahid Imām's narrations and an already catalogued and systemised terminology that Imām Aḥmad used. This allowed a comprehensive and complete understanding of his school and simplified the preferred opinion and final word of the school.[60]

From the most outstanding ʿulamā of this stage was Qādi Abu Yaʿlā Muḥammad bin Al-Ḥusayn bin Farrā (d. 458 AH), Abu Al-Khattāb Maḥfūẓ bin Aḥmad Al-Kalwadhāni (d. 510 AH) and Abu Al-Wafā ʿAli bin ʿAqīl (d. 514 AH). These ʿulamā relied on Imām Khallāl's works in clarifying the uṣūl of the madhhab.

These scholars also based works on the Mukhtaṣarul Khiraqi. They provided commentaries and meta-commentaries and explained the difficult terms used in it. Nearly twenty commentaries are available on it. The most well-known is "Al-Mughni" of Muwaffaq ibn Qudāma Al-Maqdasi (d. 620 AH)[61] who was the greatest sheikh of the school in his era. In this generation an outstanding figure of the school was Al-Majd ibn Taymiyyah (d. 652 AH).[62]

This stage is identified as the era of deep research and production of a many works explaining the school itself. Among the

---

[60] Muqaddima of Al-Jāmiʿ li ʿUlūmil Imām Aḥmad, vol. 1, pp. 111, 112.

[61] He studied Mukhtaṣarul Khiraqi with Shaykh ʿAbdul Qādir Jīlāni. This is why he is also very highly regarded among the Sufis.

[62] He is the grandfather of Shaykhul Islām Aḥmad bin ʿAbdul Halīm ibn Taymiyyah. The grandfather is considered a greater authority in the transmission of the madhhab than the grandson.

researchers were the likes of Shaykhul Islām Aḥmad bin ʿAbdul Halīm ibn Taymiyyah (d. 728 AH), Shamsuddīn Muḥammad bin Abu Bakr ibn Qayyim Al-Jawziyyah (d. 751 AH), Shamsuddīn Muḥammad bin Mufliḥ (d. 763 AH), ʿAbdur Raḥmān bin Aḥmad bin Rajab Al-Ḥanbali (d. 794 AH) and Burhānuddīn Ibrāhīm bin Muḥammad ibn Mufliḥ (d. 884 AH).

4th Stage: Stabilisation and maturing of the madhhab: 885 AH onwards

This is the last stage and continues until today. It is referred to as the "era of the Mutaakhkhirīn" or "later era authorities of the school". The school became stable and firm in this stage based on the works of the previous stage whether it be in masāil or principles. In this phase, only explanatory notes on texts are provided. Commentaries, simplification, footnotes, individual opinions on single issues are also given by scholars and explanations of a preference of a non-dominant opinion of Imām Aḥmad on single issues. However, a vast majority of the work is simply the transmission of the previous works. At this point, the school has crystallised and major shifts or ijtihād are no longer required as were in the past.[63]

Among the most outstanding scholars of this stage are Abu Ḥasan ʿAli bin Sulaymān Al-Mardāwi (d. 885 AH), Yūsuf bin ʿAbdul Hādi (d. 909 AH), Mūsa bin Aḥmad Al-Ḥajjāwi (d. 968 AH), Muḥammad bin Aḥmad Al-Futūḥi (d. 972 AH), Marʿī bin Yūsuf Al-Karmi (d. 1033 AH) and Mansūr bin Yūnus Al-Buhūti (d. 1051 AH).

This stage continues today in the form of the efforts of individual scholars in the revitalization of the school through research work, the authoring of books and the teaching of established

[63] Al-Madkhal Al-Mufaṣṣal ilā Fiqhil Imām Aḥmad bin Ḥanbal, vol. 1, p. 136; Muqaddima of Al-Jāmiʿ li ʿUlūmil Imām Aḥmad, vol. 1, p. 309.

foundational texts. Many organisations are also involved in academic research, including various Islamic institutions in the Arabian Peninsula, in preserving the school by re-publishing older works and conducting research into the masāil and uṣūl of the madhhab.[64]

[64] Al-Madkhal Al-Mufaṣṣal ilā Fiqhil Imām Aḥmad bin Ḥanbal, vol. 1, p. 136; Muqaddima of Al-Jāmi' li 'Ulūmil Imām Aḥmad, vol. 1, p. 391

Appendix 3: General principles of deriving rulings in the madhhab

The uṣūl upon which Imām Aḥmad derived his rulings does not differ from the other madhhabs except in the order in which the established sources of law are preferred. Imām Aḥmad based his methodology on:

1. Naṣṣ[65] or foundational text: i.e. the noble Qurān and rigorously authenticated Prophetic sunna. According to Imām Aḥmad, both these sources are equal as a source for deriving the rulings. However, the text of the Qurān is more reliable than the text of the sunna.

If a naṣṣ is found, then the fatwa is based on it and no opinion or analogy will be considered, even if the opinion is of a ṣaḥābi (which contradicts the naṣṣ) and that too with no differences among the ṣaḥāba. As lack of differences with others, when one disagrees with naṣṣ is not consensus or ijmāʿ.[66]

Ishāq bin Hāni has narrated that "it was said to Abu ʿAbdullah i.e.

---

[65] Qurān and Sunna are mentioned first out of respect and that all other dalīls thereafter are based on them. According to the research of the later-era scholars of the Ḥanbali school, the predominant order of sources in deriving rulings by Imām Aḥmad was:

1. Ijmāʿ
2. Qurān and Sunna Mutawātirah
3. Āḥād sunna in order of the categories within it i.e. ṣaḥīḥ lithatihi, ṣaḥīḥ lighayrihi, ḥasan lithatihi and ḥasan lighayrihi, mursal and so on.
4. Sayings of Ṣaḥāba
5. Qiyās.

Further details of the order of sources can be found in: Rawḍatun Nāẓir wa Jannatul Munāẓir, Ibn Qudāma, vol. 2, pp. 389-390; Qawāʿidul Usūl wa Maʿāqidul Fuṣūl, Ṣafiuddīn Al-Ḥanbali, p. 26, At-Taḥbīr Sharḥut Taḥrīr, Mardāwi, vol. 8, p. 4121; Al-Kawkabul Munīr Sharḥ Mukhtaṣar Al-Taḥrīr, Futuḥi, vol. 4, pp. 600-605; Al-Madkhal ilā Madhhabil Imām Aḥmad bin Ḥanbal, p.208.

[66] Iʿlāmul Muwaqqiʿīn ʿAn Rabbil ʿĀlamīn, Ibn Qayyim, vol. 1, pp. 29, 30; Al-Madkhal ilā Madhhabi Imām Aḥmad bin Ḥanbal, p. 48; Usūl Madhhabil Imām Aḥmad bin Ḥanbal, Turki, p. 106.

Imām Aḥmad that a man (a jurist or mufti) is among his people and he is asked about a matter in which there is a difference of opinion?" He replied "He should give fatwa in agreement (i.e. not differ from it in any way) with the Qurān and Sunna. And what is in conflict with Qurān and Sunna should be abstained from."[67]

Muḥammad bin Al-Ḥakam narrated that Imām Aḥmad said "... and as for a ruling based on abandoning what is narrated from the Prophet ﷺ for a conflicting narration or opinion of a ṣaḥābi or tābiʿī, then this ruling is not to be accepted over the former, as this would be unfair and over-interpretation of the sunna. Saʿd bin Ibrāhīm has narrated from Al-Qāsim who narrated from ʿĀisha رضي الله عنها, who said that the Messenger of Allāh ﷺ said "that whoever acts upon an action and our matter is not on it (i.e. not according to the Prophet's ﷺ teaching) than it is to be rejected".[68] Abu ʿAbdullah said "whoever does an action in conflict with what is narrated from Nabi ﷺ or in conflict with the sunna, then it is to be rejected."[69]

Al-Athram said "I saw and heard Abu ʿAbdullah Aḥmad bin Ḥanbal in regards to masāil. If there was anything in any issue established directly from Rasulullah ﷺ then he would not take anything from ṣaḥāba or those afterwards in opposition to it (i.e. sunna)."[70]

2. Ijmāʿ or consensus is the agreement of the mujtahids of this ummah in any single period after the passing away of Rasulullah ﷺ.[71]

Ijmāʿ is a primary source of deriving rulings according to Imām Aḥmad. Its significance is established from naṣṣ itself, as has been related by his students.

---

[67] Iʿlāmul Muwaqqiʿīn ʿAn Rabbil ʿĀlamīn, Ibn Qayyim, vol. 1, p. 31.
[68] Saḥīh Bukhāri, 2550; wording of Saḥīh Muslim, 1718.
[69] Fatāwa Kubra, Ibn Taymiyya, vol. 6, p. 217.
[70] Al-Faqīh wal Mutafaqqih, Khatīb Baghdādi, vol. 1, p. 220; Al-Musawwada, Taymiyyah Family, p. 248.
[71] Rawḍatun Nāẓir wa Jannatul Munāẓir, vol.1, pp. 423; Al-Kawkabul Munīr Sharḥ Mukhtaṣar At-Taḥrīr, vol. 1, p. 219.

Qāḍi Abu Ya'lā said "ijmā' is absolute evidence. It is compulsory to act according to it and ḥarām to be in conflict or opposition to it, as the umma will never agree on error. Imām Aḥmad stated this in the narration of 'Abdullah (his son) and Abu Al-Ḥārith: 'Regarding the Sahabah if they disagreed then none of their words are disregarded. Do you see if they agreed or had ijmā' (here Imām Aḥmad explicitly mentions ijmā' and discussed when ijmā' is not negated by any ṣaḥābi having a different view), can anyone then disregard their sayings? To do so (i.e. to disregard their sayings) is a corruption and it is the view of the people of (blameworthy) innovation. No-one should disregard anything from the sayings of the Ṣaḥaba (even) if they disagreed."[72]

Narrations that show that Imām Aḥmad rejected ijmā' are explained by Ḥanbali imāms as being attributed to his piety and utmost fear of Allāh and his cautiousness regarding the possibility of a mujtahid somewhere having a different view and hence ijmā' not being properly and truly established. He felt that it might be impossible to establish ijmā' after the era of the ṣaḥāba due to the large number of mujtahids and the distances between them and their countries.[73] However, those statements should not be misunderstood as an outright opposition to ijmā' as a source of law; rather they should be construed as Imām Aḥmad's questioning whether or not ijmā' has been in fact established.

3. Fatwas of Ṣaḥāba - Whenever, Imām Aḥmad found a fatwa of a ṣaḥābi of Nabi ﷺ and no difference was found with other companions, then he would not look elsewhere. According to him, this fatwa was preferable to forming a ra'y (independent opinion) or referring to the a'māl (action) of the people of Madīnah (as

[72] Al-'Udda fi Uṣūlil Fiqh, Qāḍi Abu Ya'lā, vol. 4, pp. 1058-1059.

[73] Al-'Udda fi Uṣūlil Fiqh, vol. 4, pp. 1059-1061; Al-Musawwada, p. 316; I'lāmul Muwaqqi'īn 'An Rabbil 'Ālamīn, vol. 1, p. 30; Mafātīḥul Fiqhul Ḥanbali, vol. 1, pp. 371, 373; Usūl Madhhabil Imām Aḥmad bin Ḥanbal, pp. 351 onwards.

Imām Mālik did)[74] or qiyās or a ḥadīth mursal (a ḥadīth in which the ṣaḥābi is omitted in the chain of narration), or a ḍaʿīf or weak chain of narration of a ḥadīth.[75] Some of the great imāms of the Ḥanbali school considered the fatwa of ṣaḥāba (with no differences) as ijmāʿ.[76]

Imām Abu Dawūd Sijistāni quoted Imām Aḥmad as saying "I have never replied to a religious ruling except with a ḥadīth from the Prophet ﷺ. If I find a solution in the ḥadīth or a narration from a ṣaḥābi or a tābiʿī (successors or followers of the ṣaḥāba), then I don't rely on anybody else. If I don't find anything from Rasulullah ﷺ, I then check from the four rightly guided khalīfas i.e. Abu Bakr, ʿUmar, ʿUthmān and Ali رضي الله عنهم. If I cannot find anything from the khalīfas, then I check with the most senior ṣaḥābi after them and I go through the ṣaḥāba giving preference to the most senior. If I cannot find a ruling then I refer to the tābiʿīn and then the tabiʿtābiʿīn (successors or followers of the tābiʿīn)." [77]

Muḥammad bin Al-Ḥakam narrated from Imām Aḥmad that he said "If the companions of Rasulullah ﷺ differed on a matter, and a man selected one of those differing opinions, the truth from Allāh has to be only one. The man will make ijtihād i.e. exert himself in trying to discern the stronger of the differing opinions without knowing which is absolutely right or wrong." He further states "if the ṣaḥāba differed and someone was to take the opinion of a ṣaḥābi, while another person took the opinion of a tābiʿī which differed with ṣaḥāba, then the truth is with the ṣaḥābi and the opinion of the tābiʿī is seen as an erroneous interpretation."[78]

If ṣaḥāba differed on a ruling, then that opinion is selected which

---

[74] One of the principles of the Māliki Madhhab is using the action of the early Muslims of Madīnah as a source of fiqh.

[75] Iʿlāmul Muwaqqiʿīn ʿAn Rabbil ʿĀlamīn, vol. 1, p. 31; Al-Madkhal ilā Madhhabi Imām Aḥmad bin Ḥanbal, p. 49; Mafātīḥul Fiqhul Ḥanbali, vol. 1, p. 374; Usūl Madhhabil Imām Aḥmad bin Ḥanbal, p. 449.

[76] Al-ʿUdda fi Uṣūlil Fiqh, vol. 4, p. 1170.

[77] Al-Musawwada, p. 301.

[78] Fatāwa Kubra, vol. 6, pp. 216, 217.

is closest to the naṣṣ i.e. to the text of the Qurān and Sunnah.[79] However, if none of the ṣaḥāba's opinions can be corroborated by naṣṣ, then no preference is given to any particular opinion and they are treated as equally valid.[80]

Al-Marwazi has narrated from Imām Aḥmad that he said "when the ṣaḥāba differ then look at that which among their opinion is closest to Qurān and Sunnah."[81]

4. Using a mursal ḥadīth or ḍaʿīf (weak) ḥadīth if there is nothing of a similar or higher source that can refute that action.

Mursal-Ḥadīth: this is a narration attributed to the Prophet of Allāh ﷺ by omitting the name of the ṣaḥābi who narrated the ḥadīth. This is the definition according to the muḥadīththīn.

According to the uṣūl (of fiqh) scholars, mursal-ḥadīth can be generalised to non-ṣaḥāba as well. They define it as a narration attributed to Rasulullah ﷺ by anyone other than ṣaḥāba and it can be in any era by simply saying the "Prophet ﷺ said".[82]

As for using acceptable ḍaʿīf-ḥadīth to derive rulings, then that which does not have severe weakness, or a bāṭil (false) attribution or munkar (rejected status) nor any narration that has a narrator accused of lying, will be considered.[83] But, if there is no authentic

---

[79] Al-ʿUdda fi Uṣūlil Fiqh, vol. 4, pp. 1105, 1208; Al-Musawwada, p. 291; Usūl Madhhabil Imām Aḥmad bin Ḥanbal, p. 451.

[80] Iʿlāmul Muwaqqiʿīn ʿAn Rabbil ʿĀlamīn, vol. 1, p. 31.

[81] Similar narrations are narrated from the Imām Aḥmad by Yūsuf Bin Mūsa and Abu Ḥārith. See: Al-ʿUdda fi Uṣūlil Fiqh, vol. 4, p. 1105.

[82] Taḥbīr Sharḥut Taḥrīr, vol. 5, p. 2136; Sharḥul Kawkabul Munīr, vol. 2, p. 574; Nuzhatun Naẓr fi Tawdīḥi Nukhbatul Fikr, Ibn Ḥajr, p. 100; An-Nukat ʿalā Ibn Ṣalāḥ, Ibn Ḥajr, vol. 2, p. 543; Tadrībur Rāwi fi Sharḥ Taqrībun Nawāwi, Suyūṭi, vol. 1, p. 195.

[83] Ibn Qayyim has opined that when Imām Aḥmad refers to ḍaʿīf narrations, that it refers to ḥasān narrations. (Iʿlāmul Muwaqqiʿīn ʿAn Rabbil ʿĀlamīn, vol. 1, p. 31) However, when books of the Ḥanbali jurists such as Qāḍi Abu Yaʿlā are

ḥadīth or a ṣaḥābi's opinion or ijmāʿ opposing it, then to practice upon it is preferred over a ruling derived by qiyās.[84]

Imām Aḥmad said as narrated by Al-Athram: "If a ḥadīth is narrated from the Prophet ﷺ with a weakness in its chain of narration, we will still accept it as long as there is nothing stronger than it that contradicts it. We will use a mursal- ḥadīth as long as there is nothing stronger than it, that is opposing it."[85]

He also said as quoted by Faḍl ibn Ziyād "The mursal narrations of Saʿīd ibn Musayyab are the most authentic mursal narrations. There is no problem with the mursal narrations of Ibrāhīm. The weakest mursal narrations are those of Al-Ḥasan and ʿAtā bin Abi Rabāḥ. Both of them narrated from everyone (i.e. without being discerning of authenticity)."[86]

Imām Aḥmad's son ʿAbdullah has narrated from his father "my method does not oppose those aḥādīth classified as weak, as long as there is nothing on that issue that contradicts it."[87] ʿAbdullah also said "I heard my father say a ḍaʿīf ḥadīth is more beloved to me than an opinion."

He also asked his father that "if a man is in a land and some matter arises and no one except a narrator of the aḥādīth, in respect of whom one cannot discern the authenticity of his narrations is found and a person who exercise his ra'y (who uses his opinion and logic) are found, then the narrator of the aḥādīth should be asked and not the person of opinion. A weak ḥadīth is better than a

---

examined, then it becomes evident that Ibn Qayyim is only referring to the analysis of the Aṣḥābul Ḥadīth and not the verdict of the fuqahā or jurists, who will still derive ruling based on a ḍaʿīf narration as long as it does not contradict a stronger proof. (Al-Musawwada, pp. 246-249)

[84] Al-Musawwada, p. 250; Iʿlāmul Muwaqqiʿīn ʿAn Rabbil ʿĀlamīn, vol. 1, p. 31; Al-Madkhal ilā Madhhabi Imām Aḥmad bin Ḥanbal, pp. 49, 50; Usūl Madhhabil Imām Aḥmad bin Ḥanbal, pp. 303 onwards, 328 onwards.

[85] Al-Faqīh wal Mutafaqqih, vol. 1, p. 220; Al-Musawwada, p. 248.

[86] Al-ʿUdda fi Uṣūlil Fiqh, vol. 3, p. 907; Al-Musawwada, p. 227.

[87] Sharḥul Kawkabul Munīr, vol. 2, p. 573.

strong opinion."[88]

5. Qiyās – Analogy: Qiyās is to be only derived from a principle based on a source that exists in the naṣṣ and that the derived ruling is similar to that in all situations. Qiyās is also called 'illah or underlying cause. Ḥusayn bin Ḥassān has said that "qiyās is the comparing of a new issue against an original ruling and it resembles the original in all its states."[89]

As for what is narrated regarding qiyās, Bakr ibn Muḥammad narrated via his father that Imām Aḥmad said "one cannot do without qiyās. It is upon every ruler and judge that people will seek them out for rulings, they must use analogy and look for similarities in prior rulings, as was done by 'Umar bin Khattāb ﵁ when he ordered his judge Shurayḥ to use analogy i.e. compare new cases to prior ones."[90]

However, qiyās cannot be relied upon for deriving rulings unless absolutely necessary i.e. in the absence of naṣṣ from the Qurān, sunna, saying of ṣaḥābi or a mursal or weak narration.[91]

Maymūni narrated that he asked Imām Shāfi'ī about qiyās. He replied "in necessity, I like it."[92]

Abu Hārith As-Sāigh narrated from Imām Aḥmad who mentioned the Ashāb ur Ra'y and refuted them. He said "What is the need for

---

[88] I'lāmul Muwaqqi'īn 'An Rabbil 'Ālamīn, vol. 1, p. 77; Al-'Udda fi Uṣūlil Fiqh, vol. 3, pp. 937-940, the discussion therein contains numerous narrations proving Imām Aḥmad's derivation of rulings based on ḍa'īf narrations.

[89] Al-Musawwada, p. 372.

[90] Al-'Udda fi Uṣūlil Fiqh, vol. 4, p. 1280.

[91] Al-Musawwada, p. 370; I'lāmul Muwaqqi'īn 'An Rabbil 'Ālamīn, vol. 1, p. 32; Al-Madkhal ilā Madhhabi Imām Aḥmad bin Ḥanbal, p. 50; Mafātīḥul Fiqhul Ḥanbali, vol. 1, pp. 378, 379.

[92] Al-Musawwada, p. 367.

opinion and analogy, when the text can suffice you?"[93]

6. Istiḥsān – juristic preference. This refers to the setting aside of an established qiyās in favour of an alternative stronger proof of a mujtahid. According to some of the fuqahā, it is leaving one qiyās for a stronger qiyās. This type of istiḥsān is reliable according to Imām Aḥmad because it is supported by dalīl or evidence. However, he has rejected it, if it does not have a sound basis and it is following one's base desires.[94] As for what has been narrated from him in regards to istiḥsān, Maymūni has quoted him saying that "I give juristic preference (astaḥsinu) to tayammum for every ṣalāt, but according to qiyās, tayammum takes the place of water and therefore the tahāra state breaks when one breaks their wuḍu or finds water."[95]

Al-Marwazi has narrated that Imām Aḥmad said "it is permissible to buy the sawād lands[96], but not permissible to sell it." It was said to him "how can you purchase from one that does not own it?" He said "Qiyās is as you say but this is istiḥsān."[97]

Qāḍi Abu Ya'lā defined istiḥsān as "the abandonment of one ruling in favour of another ruling that is more relevant to the case in question." This preference for one ruling to another had to be established on the basis of one or more of the following: the Quran, the Sunnah, or ijmā'." From this in can be understood that it is a subsidiary dalīl to the three aforementioned.

7. Istiṣḥāb – presumption of continuity. Ibn Al-Qayyim defined it

---

[93] Al-'Udda fi Uṣūlil Fiqh, vol. 4, p. 1282.
[94] Al-'Udda fi Uṣūlil Fiqh, vol. 4, p. 1604; Al-Musawwada, pp. 451-452; Rawḍatun Nāẓir wa Jannatul Munāẓir, vol. 2, p. 31; Mafātīḥul Fiqhul Ḥanbali, vol. 1, pp. 381; Usūl Madhhabil Imām Aḥmad bin Ḥanbal, p. 575.
[95] Al-'Udda fi Uṣūlil Fiqh, vol. 5, p. 1604; At-Tamhīd, Abu Khattāb, vol. 4, p. 87.
[96] This refers to the lands between Kūfa and Baṣra which 'Umar ؓ made public lands for the long-term benefit of the Muslims. In this case, Imām Aḥmad stated that Istiḥsān is applied to permit the purchase in the same way that copies of the Quran are permitted to be purchased despite the ban on their sale. Islamic Legal Theory, Mashood A. Baderin, refer to endnote 81.
[97] Al-'Udda fi Uṣūlil Fiqh, vol. 5, p. 1604.

as being the continuation of what is established or the negation of what does not exist,[98] i.e. it is that the judgement, negative or positive, continues until there is evidence of a change of state. This continuation is not proved by positive evidence, but by the absence of the existence of negating evidence.[99]

It is evidence according to Imām Aḥmad, in the absence of a proof from naṣṣ or ijmāʿ, or speech of ṣaḥāba or their fatwas, or qiyās. It can be used as proof as long as it is not negated by the former proofs.[100]

Imām Aḥmad's son Sāliḥ and Yūsuf bin Mūsa have both narrated from the Imām that not to set aside khums or one fifth[101] of the spoils of war from salab[102] because there is no narration that included salab in khums.[103] Qāḍi Abu Yaʿlā said "the absence of sharīʿa evidence is a means to continue on the original condition of not including salab as khums (thus paying it as khums after collecting it)."[104]

Al-Athram and Ibn Badīna have narrated in regards to lost jewellery that is found. Does the finder now own it? Imām Aḥmad has said on the issue "the ḥadīth (on becoming owner of lost property) is only about dinārs and dirhams."[105] Qāḍi Abu Yaʿlā elaborating on this said "he prevented ownership of lost jewellery, so the original condition is to continue i.e. non-ownership, as there

---

[98] Iʿlāmul Muwaqqiʿīn ʿAn Rabbil ʿĀlamīn, vol. 1, p. 339.

[99] Majmuʿāl Fatāwa, vol. 11, p. 342.

[100] Al-ʿUdda fi Uṣūlil Fiqh, vol. 4, pp. 1262-1263; Al-Musawwada, p. 488; Al-Madkhal ilā Madhhabi Imām Aḥmad bin Ḥanbal, p. 144; Mafātīḥul Fiqhul Ḥanbali, vol. 1, p. 382; Usūl Madhhabil Imām Aḥmad bin Ḥanbal, p. 423.

[101] Khums or one fifth was set aside for the khalīfa or sultān.

[102] Salab refers to spoils of war that consist of the animals, saddle, reigns, armour, weapons and all equipment used in war. (Muʿjam Lughatil Fuqahā, p. 296)

[103] Al-ʿUdda fi Uṣūlil Fiqh, vol. 4, p. 1263.

[104] Al-ʿUdda fi Uṣūlil Fiqh, vol. 4, p. 1263.

[105] Al-ʿUdda fi Uṣūlil Fiqh, vol. 4, p. 1264.

is no dalīl to refute this and that taking ownership has only been narrated about dirhams and dinārs."[106]

8. Sadd uth tharāiʿ – Obstructing the means. This refers to the prevention of something apparently permissible, if it leads to committing what is ḥarām.[107] This is based on the principle of the sharīʿa which considers maqāsid (objectives) and intentions and that consequence of actions are a considered objective in shariah.[108]

Under sadd uth tharāiʿ also falls ḥiyal (pl. of ḥīla). It can be translated as "legal-manoeuvre"- it is that a religiously responsible person or mukallaf intends an action or speech that is contrary to its intended use under the sharīʿa. Imām Aḥmad prohibited the usage of ḥiyal in sharīʿa rulings, if the intention is contrary to the goals of what Allāh Taʿāla establishes in that sharīʿa ruling.[109] Ḥiyal are the opposite of sadd uth tharāiʿ. Sadd uth tharāiʿ closes the door of corruption in dīn and means that lead to it. Ḥiyal are ways that deceitful people open these doors.[110]

Mūsa bin Saʿīd has narrated that Imām Aḥmad said "there is no aspect of ḥiyal that is permissible".[111] The Imām's son Sāliḥ and Abu Hārith have both narrated from him that "these ḥiyal that some people have concocted intentionally to do something contrary to the intention of the ruling is ḥarām. They say we are using legal manoeuvring or ḥīla until we can do that thing. How can they make what Allāh Taʿāla made ḥarām as ḥalāl!" The Prophet ﷺ said that "Allāh Taʿāla cursed the Bani Israīl. It was forbidden for them the fat of animals, yet they melted it and sold

---

[106] Ibid.

[107] Fatāwa Kubra, Ibn Taymiyya, vol. 3, p. 256; Iʿlāmul Muwaqqiʿīn ʿAn Rabbil ʿĀlamīn, vol. 3, p. 135; Al-Madkhal ilā Madhhabi Imām Aḥmad bin Ḥanbal, p. 148.

[108] Iʿlāmul Muwaqqiʿīn ʿAn Rabbil ʿĀlamīn, vol. 3, pp. 164, 188, 194.

[109] Iʿlāmul Muwaqqiʿīn ʿAn Rabbil ʿĀlamīn, vol. 3, pp. 138, 336; Mafātīḥul Fiqhul Ḥanbali, vol. 1, p. 388.

[110] Usūl Madhhabil Imām Aḥmad bin Ḥanbal, p. 501.

[111] Fatāwa Kubra, Ibn Taymiyya, vol. 6, p. 17.

it and consumed what they earnt from it."[112] They melted it and changed its name from fat. The Prophet ﷺ also cursed the muḥallil (one who marries someone else's divorced wife so that the ex-husband can remarry her, because he has divorced her three times and is unable to marry her) and the muḥallal lahu (the ex-husband who asked for this to be done).[113] This is an example of ḥīla explicitly forbidden by Nabi ﷺ.

The previous eight sources are the main principles of Imām Aḥmad's methodology and his legal school. Even if he utilised some other uṣūl or qawā'id in deriving rulings such as masāliḥ mursalah (public interest) or 'urf (societal custom), they are not counted as principles of his madhhab according to the most authentic view nor are they an evidence in themselves. When one looks at when these other uṣūl or qawā'id are utilised, one will see they are not independent principles [114] but used as a support to the actual above enumerated principles.[115]

---

[112] Sunan, Nasāi, 4257.

[113] Fatāwa Kubra, Ibn Taymiyya, vol. 6, p. 34; Sunan, Abu Dawūd, 2076; Sunan, Tirmidhi, 1119, 1120; Sunan, Ibn Majāh, 1934, 1935.

[114] In our times, there exists a support from certain groups to "contextualise dīn" by placing masāliḥ mursalah or 'urf as a starting point of a ruling. Instead of looking for a ruling using the framework of a madhhab, these modernists will look for anything that matches a pre-determined view; an approach which has no basis in dīn. At most, masāliḥ mursalah or 'urf are a final consideration in supporting an actual source or ruling. The stronger view is that they are not sources or proofs in and of themselves according to the Ḥanbali Madhhab.

[115] Usūl Madhhabil Imām Aḥmad bin Ḥanbal, pp. 479, 599.

Appendix 4: The most well-known works of the madhhab

The Ḥanbali Madhhab is a treasure-trove of countless beneficial authored works that have transmitted the school of Imām Aḥmad bin Ḥanbal. These works comprise the legacy of his views and opinions on a large number of fiqhi issues. They show his rules of deriving from the primary sources, his perspectives on a range of issues and also the ijtihad of the Imāms of the madhhab in codifying his madhhab in accordance with his uṣūl. These works are from different generations and vary in their level of importance. However, all these texts can be traced back to three original sources:

Firstly: The books and writings of Imām Aḥmad himself.

Secondly: Books relating to individual issues narrated from Imām Aḥmad by his direct students.

Thirdly: Books that are collections of masāil narrated from the Imām. The most important of these books is Al-Jami li Masāil Imām Aḥmad by Abu Bakr Khallāl who narrated from five of his main students.

All works authored on the fiqh of the Ḥanbali Madhhab, whether they be mutūn, compendiums or commentaries, ultimately are derived from the above three sources.[116]

With the large number and differing methods of works produced (all being uniquely beneficial), it is important to establish and understand a hierarchy of these texts to gain an appreciation for how the honourable ʿulamā of the madhhab prioritised these works. Consequently, some texts have become more well-known over time than others among the Ḥanbali scholars. Also, these texts have been thoroughly researched and commentated upon to show they authentically and precisely house and convey the madhhab of Imām Aḥmad. Commentaries and meta-commentaries further support these texts. All of these important works can be categorised into four types.

---

[116] Al-Madkhal Al-Mufaṣṣal ilā Fiqhil Imām Aḥmad bin Ḥanbal, vol. 2, p. 1086.

A. Books that narrate masāil from Imām Aḥmad

These works are those in which the direct students of Imām Aḥmad have collected the sayings, opinions and fatwas of Imām Aḥmad after he was asked questions. Among these works the most well-known[117] are:

i. Masāil of Ishāq bin Mansūr Al-Kawsaj Al-Marwazi
ii. Masāil of Ṣāliḥ bin Aḥmad bin Ḥanbal
iii. Masāil of Ishāq bin Ibrāhīm bin Hāni Nisāpūri
iv. Masāil of Abu Dawūd Sulaymān bin Ash'ath As-Sijistāni
v. Masāil of Ḥarb bin Ismā'īl Al-Karmāni
vi. Masāil of 'Abdullah bin Aḥmad bin Ḥanbal

B. Books of the Early era.

The most well-known books of the madhhab in this period are:

i. Al-Jāmi' ul 'Ulūm li Imām Aḥmad, by Abu Bakr Aḥmad bin Muḥammad Al-Khallāl (d. 311 AH). This book is considered the most comprehensive in narrating the sayings, opinions and fatwas of Imām Aḥmad and of his students who have attributed them to him. There are only one or two people in the respective chains of narration.

It was a voluminous work consisting of twenty volumes. All subsequent writers of mutūn, commentaries and primary texts afterwards relied upon it in formulating their texts. However, the book does not contain every issue narrated from Imām Aḥmad.[118]

Many chapters of the book have remained preserved intact to this

---

[117] The titles mentioned here are only of those who were prolific in transmission from Imām Aḥmad. These works are well-known and utilised among the researchers.
[118] Al-Madkhal Al-Mufaṣṣal ilā Fiqhil Imām Aḥmad bin Ḥanbal, vol. 2, pp. 669, 670.

day and serves as a great benefit to researchers and students, including:[119]

a. The book on public endowments;

b. The book on hair grooming;

c. The book on the rulings of women; and

d. The book on rulings of the communities (living in Muslim lands), apostates, heretics and public abandoners of prayers and other obligations.

ii. Mukhtaṣarul Al-Khiraqi, by Abu Qāsim ʻUmar bin Ḥusayn Al-Khiraqi (d. 334 AH). This is the first matn (a conspectus or compact summary of a larger text) of the madhhab and the most well-known. The author relied upon narrating the strongest and final opinion of Imām Aḥmad on every issue.

It became well known because ulama of the madhhab served it by their commentaries, meta-commentaries, and glosses until its commentaries reached more than three hundred in number.[120]

C. Books of the Middle Era

1. Books of Ibn Qudāma- the most well-known books of the madhhab in this period are the books of Abu Muḥammad Muwaffaquddīn ʻAbdullah bin Aḥmad bin Qudāma Al-Maqdasi (d. 620 AH), the most well-known of his works are four:[121]

a. ʻUmdatul Fiqh – a very concise matn for beginner students of the Ḥanbali madhhab. In this text, he only mentions the final opinion without mentioning other views of the madhhab on issues.

b. Al--Muqniʻ - a matn that is one step advanced from previous text and shows two or three views on any particular issue. But, it does not show the underlying reasons for each nor their

---

[119] Ibid, vol. 2, p. 671.

[120] Ad-Durrun Naqiy, Ibn Mibrad, p. 873.

[121] Al-Madkhal ilā Madhhabi Imām Aḥmad bin Ḥanbal, pp. 227, 231, 233; Al-Madkhal Al-Mufaṣṣal ilā Fiqhil Imām Aḥmad bin Ḥanbal, vol. 2, p. 719.

dalīl or proof. This text is to show beginners how rulings can be compared and to point out the most correct opinion from two or three different narrations on the same issue.

c. **Al-Kāfi** –an intermediate level text that shows the final opinion with their perspective sources or dalīls. However, sometimes two or three different views on an issue are also mentioned for the student to develop a deeper fiqh understanding.

d. **Al-Mughni fi Sharḥil Khiraqi** – arguably his most extensive and well-known work. In it, Ibn Qudāma comments on the matn of Khiraqi and clarifies other issues as well. He shows the difference of opinion not only within the madhhab, but also external to the madhhab along with reasonings and proofs. There are arguments and counter-arguments also expressed and his personal view on issues including where he felt matters should be left open.

2. **Al-Muḥarrar Fil Fiqh** – by Abul Barakāt Majduddīn Abdus Salām ibn Taymiyyah (d. 652) – a trusted matn which expresses the most relied upon views of the madhhab. The author strove to make this text concise and free from the sources and reasonings and to authenticate the strongest narration from Imām Aḥmad. However, there are some masāil in this book regarding which there is still difference of opinion.[122]

3. **Al-Furū'** - by Abu Abdullah Shamsuddin Muḥammad bin Mufliḥ Al-Ḥanbali (d. 763 AH) - an extensive work that collects many masāil and subsidiary derived issues or furū'. It does not contain reasonings or proofs. Preference is given to the preferred view of the madhhab. However, for some issues, the differences are discussed to show why there is a preference for one view over

[122] Muqaddima of Muḥarrar fil Fiqh, Al-Majd Ibn Taymiyya, p. 1; Al-Madkhal ilā Madhhabi Imām Aḥmad bin Ḥanbal, p. 232; Al-Madkhal Al-Mufaṣṣal ilā Fiqhil Imām Aḥmad bin Ḥanbal, vol. 2, p. 712.

another and this is usually contrasting the other three madhhabs. He also relies on his shaykh, Ibn Taymiyya on certain issues when it comes to these differences.[123]

4. **Al-Mubdi' Fi Sharḥil Muqni'** - by Abu Ishāq Burhānuddīn Ibrāhīm bin Muḥammad Ibn 'Abdullah bin Mufliḥ (d. 884 AH) - a commentary on Al-Muqni' by Muwaffaq ibn Qudāma Al-Maqdasi. He clarifies its masāil and rulings with proofs from the Qurān and Sunnah. He mentions Imām Aḥmad's differing narrations on issues and differing sayings of ṣaḥāba. He gives preference to one view over others, removes differences and affirms which issues do not give rise to differences.[124]

D. Books of the latter era.

The most well-known books of the madhhab in this period are:

1. **Al-Inṣāf fi Ma'rifati Ar-Rājiḥ min Khilāf** by 'Alāuddīn 'Ali bin Sulaymān Al-Mardāwi (d. 885 AH) - based on the Muqni' of ibn Qudāma Maqdasi with additional masāil missed in Muqni'. He clarifies beneficial points on some issues, cautions in respect of other issues and gives a conclusive verdict and argument on yet other issues that gave rise to differences. For this reason, it is considered one of the most comprehensive works of the madhhab, as it gathers all contradictory narrations of Imām Aḥmad, clarifies them, shows the various viewpoints, explores different possibilities and finally affirms and concludes with that which is most correct of the differences and what is the final position of the madhhab. He refers to all prior references of the madhhab whether they be a matn, commentary or a meta commentary. It is a book that allows one to be independent of all books of the madhhab before it.[125]

---

[123] Al-Madkhal ilā Madhhabi Imām Aḥmad bin Ḥanbal, p. 235; Al-Madkhal Al-Mufaṣṣal ilā Fiqhil Imām Aḥmad bin Ḥanbal, vol. 2, pp. 754, 755.

[124] Muqaddima of Al-Mubdi' Fi Sharḥil Muqni', Burhānuddīn ibn Mufliḥ, vol. 1, p. 13.

[125] Al-Madkhal Al-Mufaṣṣal ilā Fiqhil Imām Aḥmad bin Ḥanbal, vol. 2, pp. 729, 730.

2. Al-Iqnāʿ li Tālibil Intifāʿ by Sharfuddīn Abu Najā Mūsa bin Aḥmad bin Mūsa Al-Ḥajjāwi (d. 968 AH) - published in four volumes. The author borrowed the majority of it from the book Al-Mustawʿib by As-Sāmurrai.[126]

This is an exceptional text, primarily due to the large number of masāil covered in simple and clear language. It is also very concise in that it is free from narrations, evidences and reasonings. The focus is on the final word of the madhhab i.e. the preferred opinion. However, in some instances a contradictory opinion is mentioned if it has strength or where an issue is left without judgment and there is no clear proof to affirm its correctness.

Iqnaʿ is an important matn from which later ḥanbali scholars taught and upon which they commentated, wrote footnotes and summarised into concise texts and of which they explained its obscure language until it became a text of fatāwa and courts.[127]

The most well-known and well written commentary of Iqnaʿ is Kashshāful Qināʿ by the great researcher and examiner of the madhhab, Shaykh Mansūr al Buhūti (d. 1051 AH).[128]

3. Muntahal Irādāt fil Jāmiʿ baynal Muqniʿ wan Tanqīḥ wa Ziyādāt by Abu Bakr Taqiuddīn Muḥammad bin Aḥmad Al-Futūḥi who is better known as Ibn Najjār (d. 972 AH) - a book that combines two important books of the madhhab i.e. Muqniʿ of Ibn Qudāma and Al-Tanqīḥul Mushbiʿ of ʿAlāuddīn Mardāwi. The second book is a compilation of new derived rulings from the first book. Al-Futūḥi

---

126 Ibn Badrān says in Al-Madkhal, p. 234 "He has definitely imitated the author of Mustawʿib. Actually, most of it is from Mustawʿib, Al-Muḥarrar, Al-Furūʿ and Al-Muqniʿ."

127 Muqaddima of Al-Iqnāʿ li Ṭālibil Intifāʿ, Al-Ḥajjāwi, vol. 1, p. 2; Al-Madkhal ilā Madhhabi Imām Aḥmad bin Ḥanbal, pp. 234, 138; Al-Madkhal Al-Mufaṣṣal ilā Fiqhil Imām Aḥmad bin Ḥanbal, vol. 2, pp. 765-766.

128 Muqaddima of Al-Iqnāʿ li Ṭālibil Intifāʿ, vol. 1, p. 2; Al-Madkhal ilā Madhhabi Imām Aḥmad bin Ḥanbal, pp. 234, 138; Al-Madkhal Al-Mufaṣṣal ilā Fiqhil Imām Aḥmad bin Ḥanbal, vol. 2, pp. 765-766.

combined both texts and all their masāil and simplified the presentation of the rulings.

This book is considered one of the most important books for later Ḥanbali scholars because fatwas are based upon it and it is used as a reference in court rulings. It is a compilation of the most preferred and final positions of the madhhab.[129]

4. Ghāyatul Muntahā fil Jāmi‘ baynal Iqnā‘ wal Muntahā by Mar‘ī bin Yūsuf Al-Karmi (d. 1033 AH) - a book that combines two important books of the later Ḥanbalis i.e. Iqnā‘ of Ḥajjāwi and Muntahā Irādāt of Ibn Najjār. The understanding of the madhhab rests upon these two books. Also fatwas and court ruling were based upon them, when they were compiled.

This book is famous for mentioning the final points of the madhhab. It is the relied upon text when one seeks to know the most correct view in instances where there is a difference on an issue between Iqnā and Muntahā.[130] Saffārīni said, on his death bed to one of his students from Najd, "It is necessary that you follow what is in two books; Iqnā‘ and Muntahā, if they differ then look at what the author of Al-Ghāya gives preference to."[131]

---

[129] Al-Madkhal ilā Madhhabi Imām Aḥmad bin Ḥanbal, p. 237; Al-Madkhal Al-Mufaṣṣal ilā Fiqhil Imām Aḥmad bin Ḥanbal, vol. 2, pp. 778, 779.

[130] Al-Madkhal ilā Madhhabi Imām Aḥmad bin Ḥanbal, p. 239; Al-Madkhal Al-Mufaṣṣal ilā Fiqhil Imām Aḥmad bin Ḥanbal, vol. 2, p. 786.

[131] Muqaddima of Kashshāful Qinā‘, vol. 1, p. 12.

Appendix 5: Some terminology used by the Ḥanbalis

As with all Madhhabs, the Ḥanbali Madhhab uses specific language or terminology to express fiqhi understandings. These terms differentiate between the speech of Imam Ahmad and other Imams of the Madhhab, their ijtihād or juristic deductions, their derivation of principles and juristic philosophy for masāil based on the principles of the madhhab, where the Imām had not provided a direct ruling for an issue.

The Ḥanbali scholars referred to specific authored works or Imāms by specific terms or titles. Furthermore, specific terms are utilised in the madhhab to clarify or determine the soundest ruling or narration.

All these terms are used as a shorthand so reference to scholars and books can be briefly mentioned without long repetitions.

These terms can be divided in three categories:

1. Terms to differentiate between sayings of the Imām and sayings of his followers.

a. Riwāyah or narration - it is a ruling narrated from Imām Aḥmad by one of his students. It of two types:

> **i. Ṣārīḥ or explicit** – it is an utterance of the Imām which clarifies a ruling of an issue that cannot have any other possible interpretation. The Ḥanbalis quote these using words such as naṣṣan, naṣṣa ʿalayhi, al-manṣūṣ ʿalayhi, al manṣūṣ ʿanhu, ʿanhu, rawāhul jamāʿah.[132]
>
> **ii. Tanbīh or cautioning** – a narrator relates something from the Imām according to what he has understood from the Imām's speech, ishāra (indication) or imāʾ (hint) (All of these ways are implicit as opposed to ṣārīḥ). They are mentioned in

[132] Al-Inṣāf fi Maʿrifati Ar-Rājiḥ min Khilāf, Al-Mardāwi, vol. 1, p. 19, vol. 12, p. 240; Al-Madkhal Al-Mufaṣṣal ilā Fiqhil Imām Aḥmad bin Ḥanbal, vol. 1, p. 173.

the texts using words such as awma'a ilayhi, ashāra ilayhi, dalla kalāmuhu ʿalayhi, tawaqqafa fīhi, sakata ʿanhu.[133]

b. Wajh or view – it is a transmitted ruling in a mas'ala from some of the aṣḥāb that are mujtahids in the madhhab. This ruling will be on the qawā'id and usūl of the Imām and it can also be different to the qawā'id of the Imām if it is supported by a dalīl.[134]

c. Al-iḥtimāl or leeway – the potential of a mas'ala of having a ruling or ḥukm other than the ruling that is quoted already. This is done due to the proof of the first ruling being flawed or weak in relation to the proof for the second ruling or that both rulings are equal in strength.

It is similar to wajh, except that wajh is directly linked to fatwas while iḥtimāl is not. However, if a fatwa is given based on it, then it becomes a wajh of the one who issued the fatwa.[135]

d. Takhrīj or extracting from a naṣṣ – transmission of a ruling to a mas'ala from a naṣṣ and then applying it to what resembles it and showing the similarities. This cannot be achieved until both issues, sourced or derived, are understood well. Takhrīj can be from the Imām's qawā'id kulliyyah (Islamic legal maxims) or sharīʿa in general or the use of intellect.[136]

e. Ẓāhirul Madhhab or the apparent Madhhab - it is a well-known and obvious ruling of the school.[137]

f. Qawl or remark – includes all of the utterances of the ʿulamā of the ḥanbali madhhab in any issue. They can be attributed to the Imām as wajh, iḥtimāl or takhrīj. And it can be naṣṣ and includes

---

[133] Al-Musawwada, p. 532; Al-Inṣāf fi Maʿrifati Ar-Rājiḥ min Khilāf, vol. 12, p. 241.
[134] Al-Musawwada, p. 532; Al-Muṭliʿ, Al-Baʿli, p. 460; Al-Inṣāf fi Maʿrifati Ar-Rājiḥ min Khilāf, vol. 12, p. 256; Al-Madkhal ilā Madhhabi Imām Aḥmad bin Ḥanbal, p. 62.
[135] Al-Musawwada, p. 533; Al-Muṭliʿ, p. 461; Al-Inṣāf fi Maʿrifati Ar-Rājiḥ min Khilāf, vol. 1, p. 17; Al-Madkhal ilā Madhhabi Imām Aḥmad bin Ḥanbal, p. 63.
[136] Al-Musawwada, p. 533; Al-Inṣāf fi Maʿrifati Ar-Rājiḥ min Khilāf, vol. 17, p. 1; Al-Madkhal ilā Madhhabi Imām Aḥmad bin Ḥanbal, pp. 60, 63.
[137] Al-Muṭliʿ, p. 461.

riwāyah as well.[138]

g. Qiyās ul Madhhab or **analogy of the madhhab** – extracting a subsidiary ruling (not from the imām) based on a subsidiary issue extracted by the Imām because of a common underlying reason between the two issues.[139]

h. Tawaqquf or abstention – it is the silence of the Imām or a Mujtahid in the madhhab from issuing a ruling on a mas'ala because of conflicting dalīls or their being apparently equal to each other even though individually they are both correct and one cannot refute either of them.[140]

2. Terms that express preference or authentication of a ruling

These are terms that are used by authors and researchers to express the preferred and strongest riwāyah of the school of the Imām when there are different riwāyahs from Imām Aḥmad or different qawls and wajhs. The most important terminology[141] from these are:

a. al aṣaḥḥ, fil aṣaḥḥ, 'alal aṣaḥḥ, aṣ ṣaḥiḥ, fiṣ ṣaḥiḥ, fiṣ ṣaḥiḥ minal Madhhab, fiṣ ṣaḥiḥ 'anhu, fi aṣaḥḥil qawlayn/aqwaali/wajhayn/awjuh, al awwalu aṣaḥḥ, hiya aṣaḥḥ, al awwalu aqyasu wa aṣaḥḥ or hātha ṣaḥiḥ 'indi.
b. al mashhūr, fil mashhūr 'anhu, 'alal mashhūr or al ashharu.
c. al aẓhar, aẓharu huma, 'alal aẓhar, 'alā aẓhari hima, fil aẓhari or fi aẓhar wajhayn/awjuh.

---

138 Al-Musawwada, p. 533; Al-Inṣāf fi Ma'rifati Ar-Rājiḥ min Khilāf, vol. 12, p. 257.

139 Al-Madkhal ilā Madhhabi Imām Aḥmad bin Ḥanbal, pp. 274, 275.

140 Al-Musawwada, pp. 526, 533; Al-Madkhal ilā Madhhabi Imām Aḥmad bin Ḥanbal, p. 63; Al-Madkhal Al-Mufaṣṣal ilā Fiqhil Imām Aḥmad bin Ḥanbal, vol. 1, p. 260.

141 Al-Madkhal Al-Mufaṣṣal ilā Fiqhil Imām Aḥmad bin Ḥanbal, vol. 1, pp. 311, 312.

d. riwāyatun wāḥidatun, qawlan wāḥidan or wajhan wāḥidan.
e. bilā khilāf fil madhhab or bilā nizā'.
f. al-manṣūṣ, al madhhabul manṣūṣ, naṣṣan, naṣṣa 'alayhi, 'alayhi or wa huwa ikhtiyārul aṣḥāb.
g. awlāhuma katha, al awlā katha or huwa awlā.
h. al aqwā, fil aqwā or yuqawwā.
i. al awwalu aḥsan.
j. akhtārahu 'āmatul aṣḥāb.
k. al madhhabu katha or al madhhabu al awwalu.
l. al qiyāsu katha, fi qiyāsil madhhabi katha or al awwalu aqyasu.

In their introductions, all authors explain the terminology used in their books that express preference and how to distinguish the preferred riwāyah, wajh, qawl, takhrīj or iḥtimāl and if they use any terminology different to what is used in the madhhab, such as Abu Bakr ibn Zayd Al-Jurā'i (d. 883 AH) in his book Ghāyatul Maṭlab fi Ma'rifatul Madhhab.

3. Terms used for some of the 'ulamā of the madhhab

From among the terminology used by the authors are references to Imāms of the madhhab by their titles (by which they are commonly known). This is a shorthand, so their whole name does not need to be repeated. The most well-known names are:

Al-Qādi or the judge – Qādi Muḥammad bin Hussain bin Muḥammad bin Khalaf bin Aḥmad bin Al-Farrā, more well known as Abu Ya'lā (d. 458 AH). He is known as Qādi for the middle era until the middle of the eighth century. As for the latter-era scholars such as the authors of Iqnā' and Muntahā, Qādi refers to Qādi 'Alāuddin 'Ali bin Sulaymān Al-Mardāwi (d. 885 AH).[142]

Ash-Shaykh or the Shaykh – refers to the Muwaffaquddīn Abu

142 Al-Madkhal ilā Madhhabi Imām Aḥmad bin Ḥanbal, p. 216; Al-Madkhal Al-Mufaṣṣal ilā Fiqhil Imām Aḥmad bin Ḥanbal, vol. 1, p. 213.

Muḥammad ʿAbdullah ibn Qudāma Al-Maqdasi (d. 620 AH). He was known as *shaykh* among the middle-era ḥanbalis such as Ibn Qādi Al-Jabal (d. 771 AH), Ash-Shams Ibn Mufliḥ, Ibn Laḥḥām (d. 803 AH) and Abu Bakr bin Zayd Al-Jurāʿi. As for the latter-era ḥanbalis, *shaykh* refers to Abu ʿAbbās Aḥmad bin ʿAbdul Ḥalīm Ibn Taymiyya (d. 728 AH).[143]

Ash- Shaykhān or the Two Shaykhs – this title jointly refers to Muwaffaquddīn ʿAbdullah ibn Qudāma Al-Maqdasi (d. 620 AH) and Abu Barakāt ʿAbdus Salām bin ʿAbdullah bin Abul Qāsim bin Muḥammad bin Taymiyya (d. 652 AH).[144]

Shaykhul Islām or Shaykh of Islām - two imāms became famous with this title: Muwaffaquddīn ʿAbdullah ibn Qudāma Al-Maqdasi (d. 620 AH) and Abu ʿAbbās Aḥmad bin ʿAbdul Ḥalīm Ibn Taymiyya (d. 728 AH).[145] The latter one is more well-known by this title than the former.

Ash-Shāriḥ or the Commentator – this title applies mostly to Abu ʿUmar ʿAbdur Raḥmān ibn Muḥammad bin Aḥmad ibn Qudāma Al-Maqdasi (d. 682 AH). He was the nephew of Muwaffaquddīn ibn Qudāma.[146]

Al-Jamāʿah or the Group – this refers to seven students of Imām Aḥmad i.e. his two sons ʿAbdullah and Ṣāliḥ, Imām Aḥmad's cousin Ḥanbal, Abu Bakr Murwadhi, Ibrāhīm Ḥarbi (d. 285 AH), Abu Tālib (d. 244 AH) and Maymūni (d. 274 AH). They are intended when one comes across the expression *Rawāhul Jamāʿah* meaning "the group has narrated.

---

143 Al-Madkhal ilā Madhhabi Imām Aḥmad bin Ḥanbal, p. 216; Al-Madkhal Al-Mufaṣṣal ilā Fiqhil Imām Aḥmad bin Ḥanbal, vol. 1, pp. 201, 202.

144 Al-Madkhal ilā Madhhabi Imām Aḥmad bin Ḥanbal, p. 216.

145 Al-Madkhal Al-Mufaṣṣal ilā Fiqhil Imām Aḥmad bin Ḥanbal, vol. 1, p. 204.

146 Taṣḥīḥul Furūʿ, Al-Mardāwi, vol. 1, p. 30; Al-Inṣāf, vol. 1, p. 15; Al-Madkhal ilā Madhhabi Imām Aḥmad bin Ḥanbal, p. 216.

www.ingramcontent.com/pod-product-compliance
Lightning Source LLC
Chambersburg PA
CBHW031418290426
44110CB00011B/441
9780648247142